When Israel Is King

WHEN ISRAEL IS KING

JEROME AND JEAN THARAUD

The content of this work is in the public domain.

First Antelope Hill edition, first printing 2024.

This edition is an edited and reformatted republication of the English edition translated by Lady Whitehead from the French published by Robert M. McBride & Company, New York, 1924.

Covert art by Swifty.
Edited by T. Brock.
Layout by Sebastian Durant.

Antelope Hill Publishing | antelopehillpublishing.com

Paperback ISBBN-13: 979-8-89252-007-2
EPUB ISBN-13: 979-8-89252-008-9

CONTENTS

Introduction 1
I. The Portrait of Bismarck 3
II. A Bulwark of the West 13
III. The House of Orczi 21
IV. The Murder of Count Tisza 31
V. An Ambitious Magnate 59
VI. The End of the Hapsburgs 79
VII. Karolyi's Triumph 89
VIII. Bela Kun 105
IX. The New Jerusalem 121
X. In Rural Hungary 135
XI. The Downfall of the Soviets 149
XII. A Dialogue Without End 157
XIII. The Staff of Ahasuerus 171

— INTRODUCTION —

The present collection is due to the action of certain public-spirited Frenchmen desirous of making better known in English-speaking countries some of their foremost writers of today. They are also anxious to rehabilitate in the minds of those who are not intimately acquainted with the extraordinary richness and variety of modern French literature the foreign reputation of their country which has often suffered in the past from the translations of certain books that have attained a bubble reputation in France and abroad, by reason of the notorious nature of their contents.

All who wish to learn about the real France will find in the present series abundant examples of that sense of life and beauty that distinguishes the French genius, with its unwearying quest of lucidity and proportion (and its balanced belief in the reality of the external and internal world), and above all of that serene seriousness that made possible the miracle of the Marne and the immortal defense of Verdun.

I

— THE PORTRAIT OF BISMARCK —

One day in the autumn of 1899, a young Frenchman arrived at Budapest. No one was waiting for him at the station and he had great difficulty in extricating his luggage and in finding someone to conduct him to the house where he was expected, for, of course, he did not know a single word of Hungarian.

It is always a trying moment when one first arrives in an unknown country to which one has been led by force of circumstances, not by the mere pleasure of traveling, and when a vista of long months to be passed among people and things which chance has chosen for one stretches out ahead. My arrival in Hungary on that autumn afternoon was the crowning point of a long series of years at college, of days without light or liberty or nature, of tedious study, and of examinations without end; and the result of all this had been that one fine day the minister of public instruction sent me as a lecturer on the French language to the Budapest University. The irony of life came home to me in full when, burdened by the weight of my two portmanteaux and laboriously searching for a cab, something within me wondered whether so many hours spent in the Lycée, the Sorbonne, and in boredom, so many regulated efforts directed towards one end spread over so many years, were to culminate in landing me just here and nowhere else, at this railway station, in the center of this town, where I should one day exhibit before a small audience of a few young people the meager stock of knowledge which I had been accumulating for twenty years and which represented approximately my whole capital in life. Standing a little later in the furnished apartment which I at length reached, my luggage at my feet, I considered with comic bitterness those few square yards towards which, ever since I left Paris, and indeed long before that, ever since my childhood, destiny seemed to have impelled me. A bed, a table, two chairs, a sofa covered with American cloth, cracked in many places, a gas pipe hanging from the ceiling, ill lit (for the window looked out upon a court)—that was the sight which met my eyes. Over the bed, hung on the wall, there was a portrait of Bismarck, one of those photogravures after one of Lenbach's pictures, which at that time an enterprising publisher was spreading broadcast throughout Germany and in all the countries subject to German influence.

It was not the well-known portrait in uniform, with the iron cross and the pointed helmet; neither was it the one in which the artist has concentrated (as in Rembrandt's fashion) all the light of his canvas on the vast rock-like skull. It was not the Iron Chancellor, nor the soldier, nor the official who was portrayed in this picture, but an old man, clad like one of the middle class, his head surmounted by a broadbrimmed black hat—an East Prussian country squire, a Bismarck who might always have lived on his own land and passed his days in superintending his domains and collecting his rents. But whether or not anything wonderful had happened in the life of this personage, one felt oneself in the presence of an animal of superb race, with a powerful will firmly established in simple and ancestral ideas.

Should I keep the head of that old country gentleman, with the firm jaw, whose gaze looked out from the deep arch of his bushy eyebrows, looking down upon me from the wall of my room? Should I remain in a perpetual tête-à-tête with that enemy countenance, and have it there morning, noon, and night before my eyes, for all my life? Slowly the light waned around me and the dusk of evening enveloped the room. As darkness fell, the man with the big hat faded away on the wall.

I myself, worn out with the fatigue of unnumbered hours of journeying in a third-class carriage over half of Europe, and washed up at last, like flotsam, at the foot of that portrait, seemed to dissolve in the same darkness. Strange experience! When, a moment later, I had set alight to the gas jet hanging from the ceiling, and the man with the hat reappeared on the wall, I saw him again with pleasure. I was no longer alone in my room. That hostile, hard countenance abruptly recalled to me certain familiar thoughts. Already between him and me a colloquy had been established; his unexpected presence gave a tone and, as it were, a romantic character to my squalid arrival. Certainly I had never expected to find a host of such importance in a chance room! Thanks to him I had already experienced an emotion in this strange and mean chamber, which is to say I had begun to live. If I were to remove the picture from its place, I should not only add to the blankness of the wall, but I should rarefy the atmosphere and enlarge the desert around me. Let it be, I thought, we will live together; one never wastes one's time while in company with such a personality.

So the picture remained, and I must confess that during the four years which I passed in that room we lived very happily together. That portrait became for me a silent and eloquent companion, with whom from time to time, it was good to exchange ideas. I received many a piece of good advice from every line graven on that churlish face, which, at certain hours and under certain plays of light, took on a wonderfully shrewd look and sometimes even an air of melancholy. As a young Frenchman, trained in the ideas which were current with us at the end of the last century, I had arrived there full of the most immature political and social views; but under that stern look, certain naivetes were no longer permitted! I found myself there under the eyes of a judge and of a severe counsellor. When my thoughts floated idly on nothing in particular, I would suddenly become conscious of the clear eyes gazing at me from under the black hat. Then my vagabond spirit, which was always pursuing some romantic chimera, would return to the straight path of reality. And even without my realizing it, during the long, silent, and melancholy hours of exile, that glance reacted upon me, penetrated my inward consciousness, and helped me to see the vanity of the ideas which, in a student's lodging between the Seine and the Luxembourg, might well exercise an irresistible attraction, but which were out of place here, in the presence of that redoubtable stranger. My severe companion rescued me from the tyranny which books always exercise over the brain of a youth of twenty years (especially when, as in my case, he lived in great solitude), and taught me, without any words, the supreme power of experience and fact. For four years, I was conscious of that face, now grave, now ironic, considering the young Frenchman lost in Central Europe, reading or writing at his plain deal table. For four years that impassive face played the part of a sheepdog about my thoughts, keeping them well grouped together and preventing them from straying hither and thither. And when, after so many days passed in his company, I left Budapest and that room, where nothing had been changed since my arrival, my last look was on Bismarck's portrait which had received me there, certainly not a friendly glance, but assuredly one full of gratitude.

When I look back on the long stay I made at that time in Budapest, I say to myself, not without a trace of melancholy, that for a young man of a lively disposition there are more romantic adventures than to explain as a pedagogue one of La Fontaine's fables, a tragedy of Racine's, or "Le Neveu de Rameau." Yet, if one considers, there is a certain touch of the comic novel in the idea of earning one's livelihood by trying to persuade others that the things one loves oneself are lovable. When Don Quixote celebrated the merits of his Dulcinea, he could hardly have seemed, I imagine, more extravagant to Sancho than I must have appeared to my Hungarian students, when I unrolled before them my intellectual pack, and I have often told myself that they must secretly have thought that only my vanity as a Frenchman could have enabled me to discover in those admirable books the things which I pretended to find there. How often, while I talked to them, I thought, with a feeling of homesickness, of that cultivated Europe of the eighteenth century which had made French its natural language, and of those aristocrats who, in their lonely castles, took the same pleasure in reading our Encyclopedists, or our splendid classics, as we do ourselves! But then they had not waited till they had almost arrived at man's estate to learn our language. From their childhood upward they had heard it round them, and no learned doctor from the Sorbonne could replace some old soldier, the flotsam of the Seven Years War, who after a thousand vicissitudes had said goodbye to his Burgundy or his Normandy and had one fine day come to rest in the capacity of tutor in some noble house of the Carpathians or the Puszta. But above all, in those blessed days, the sinister German culture had not yet arisen, to throw its false weights into the light scales of the spirit.

I was conscious that some of my young Hungarians were tempted to escape to Paris and initiate themselves into a life which they instinctively guessed was more free, more joyous, and more human than the German one. Only they were poor, and the scholarships which were granted to them for the completion of their studies stipulated invariably that they should go to Leipzig, Munich, or Berlin. The funds for these scholarships were furnished by Germany, which applied to the intellectual domain the same methods from which she drew such great advantages in her worldwide commerce. Thus she opened for the benefit of Hungarian intelligence a sort of account current, with the certainty of recovering, someday, a hundred percent interest on her money.

I should indeed have been fairly uncomfortable in that university, which was more than three quarters Germanized, if I had not found among those young Magyars a spontaneity and a youthful charm which caused them to evade with a smile or by sheer idleness the gloomy German discipline. Teutonic pedantry, which has today stultified all Central Europe, did not succeed in stifling the impulsive and idyllic character of the Hungarian spirit—all that rural poetry which finds its best expression in the poems of Petöfi, and especially in the work of John Arány, the disciple of Virgil and near relation of Mistral. The thing they love and understand with all their power and ingenuity is life on the great plains, where corn and vines and maize ripen and where immense herds of cattle, horses, and sheep are pastured. On this subject they possess a charmingly fantastic literature, at the same time realistic and spiritual, in which one sees the shepherd sharing fraternal sentiments with his beasts. It never rises above the modest limits of a tale, but within those bounds it is perfect. Ah! why do these Hungarians want to think in German fashion, when they would be so charming if they remained quite simply as nature has made them! How many of them, by doing so, have lost the qualities of a race which remained close to the soil, without acquiring in exchange the painstaking virtues of the Germans—if one can describe as virtues an infinity of faults and a sad deformation of human mentality!

Today, after nearly twenty years have elapsed, I return to Budapest. On the boat which carries me down the swift current of the broad Danube, with its banks fringed with willows, those distant impressions are mingled with another recollection which dates but from yesterday: the signature at Versailles of the treaty with Hungary.

It was in the Palace of Versailles, in a long and magnificent gallery decorated with mirrors and with panels representing the fountains, the grottoes and basins of Versailles. Through the open windows one saw, beneath a rather cloudy sky, the trees and lawns of the garden, while within a fairly numerous party of men and women were moving and chattering as if they were assembled for an elegant tea party. All of a sudden, an usher announced, in resounding tones, "The Hungarian Plenipotentiaries." Then, in a silence charged with emotion, there advanced towards the horseshoe table, round which were seated about fifty diplomatists, a small group of men, their eyes fixed, their faces pale, and their carriage rather stiff. These were the men delegated by Hungary to sign, here in this hall scintillating with sunshine and full of the grace of summer, the act which took from their country two-thirds of the territory which had been hers for more than a thousand years. One stroke of the pen was about to detach from the Crown of Saint Stephen the vast range of mountains which encircles the great Hungarian plain, and the millions of inhabitants of diverse races, Slovaks, Ruthenians, Romanians, Serbs, Saxons, Tziganes, Jews, and pure Magyars—all that population which lives inextricably mixed in the Marches of Hungary. Under their faultless frock coats those plenipotentiaries seemed to me, at that moment, to resemble the burghers of Calais in their long, floating shirts, and I felt how heavily the keys which they carried must weigh in their hands. I knew the extent of their loss, and how strong was the sentiment which attached their Hungarian hearts to that millenarian domain. Charmingly romantic pictures rose in my memory: of high, silent valleys, the stampede of chamois through the snow; pine trees uprooted on the banks of torrents; ancient half-ruined castles crowning the summit of rock or forest, where heroes, whose legends were told to me, had lived; villages where poets, whose verses were recited to me, had been born; ancient patriarchal domains in which I had received hospitality. In spirit I heard something which resembled that farewell, so homely and tender, which the province of Szepes, detached from Hungarian territory by this Trianon Treaty, addressed to its old country, and of which, while writing these lines, I have the text before my eyes. "We have no intention," say these people of Szepes, "to present an account, or to strike a balance. We only take our leave. We thank you quite simply for that good white flour with which we have been nourished for a thousand years, and which has made such delicious cakes for our children. We thank you for the wine of Tokai which has flowed nowhere so abundantly as with us. We thank you for the black cherries, the juicy apricots, the luscious grapes and the good red watermelons that the women of Eger sold in the markets of our towns. We thank you for the excellent Erdötélek tobacco, which you brought us at the same time as the lilies of the valley. And you, O ancient mountains, O shining peaks above the clouds, O lovely Alpine lakes with your emerald splendors, and thou too, O powerful Magura, that holdest the tomb of Arpad, the conquering prince of our fatherland, all of you, O distant blue mountains of Szepes, stand back! Let the song of the thrush be still! Let the murmur of the forest rustle alone, let it rustle through the mountains and the valleys, let it carry our sighs to those to whom now we bid farewell!"

Meanwhile, one after another, the Plenipotentiaries had affixed their signatures at the foot of the sheet of paper. The Magyar delegates retired through the throng of spectators, who this time rose from their seats to make way for them. Outside a curt word of command was heard, followed at once by the rattle of arms: it was the guard saluting. Around us the hum of conversation had begun again. We crowded towards the buffet, and amid the sound of voices and of chairs being pushed back, I saw once more in spirit that whitewashed wall on which hung the portrait of that faraway author of this immense calamity: the man with broad-brimmed hat who had received me over there on that sad autumn evening, and whose eyes had watched over me day and night for four long years.

II

— A BULWARK OF THE WEST —

This morning I climbed the hill of Buda, from which, in old days, I had so often contemplated the beautiful landscape that unfolds itself there: a vast semicircle of wooded hills, then the bare, muddy expanse of the Danube which flows at the foot of the rock, on the further side of the river, on its flat bank, the great new town of Pest, and beyond it the never-ending plain.

When I arrived there twenty years ago, the city of Buda, seated on its narrow plateau, was a small, ancient town, entirely provincial in character, consisting of low houses, at most one story high, and nearly all plastered over with a strange yellow limewash. One looked in vain for any of those palaces which the eighteenth century had so lavishly bestowed on Prague or Vienna, with their giant caryatides, their cornices decorated with a whole population of tormented statues, and their admirable balconies—all carried out in a fine Italian style of architecture, but in a somewhat more massive manner suitably adapted to a northern climate. At Buda, the palace of a magnate was a very simple dwelling, bourgeois in style and reminding one of the country. The only touch of art was given by the porch and the armorial bearings. The Hapsburgs never did anything to make the old hill splendid. Maria Theresa, who built so much in other places, erected nothing there but a long, monotonous building, which, moreover, has been pulled down in order that the new royal castle, pretentious and heavy like a modern palace hotel, should take its place. As for the Magyar nobles whom the court attracted to Vienna, they built themselves sumptuous residences there in the neighborhood of the Hofburg and contented themselves with a modest pied-à-terre at Buda, which they inhabited on the rare occasions when the king and queen came to Hungary.

Sometimes one sees, embedded in the yellow limewash which covers these low-built houses, a relief portraying the head of a decapitated Turk, or more often one reads an inscription: "Here in 1450 lived the Despot of Bosnia," or "Here in 1388 stood the Palace of the Viceroy of the Banat," or of such and such a Balkan prince. You enter under the archway, which is large enough to allow of the passage of a carriage and pair and you find yourself in a roughly paved yard, where grass is growing; there is a well in one corner and all round it are buildings, whose old roofs, with flat tiles, incline steeply towards the ground. All that remains of the Despot of the Banat, or the Hospodar of Walachia in that enclosure, is a fragment of a Romanesque arch, a cellar, a pillar round which a vine is trained and on which a canary's cage is hung. Near these vestiges of a former age live small householders, retired public functionaries, or small artisans, leading their peaceful lives. But that Turk's head, that pillar, or that arch are sufficient to awaken the imagination of the passerby and to remind him that on this hill, which today has become so squalid, great events took place in the past. That old rock of Buda, like Marathon, Salamis, or the Catalaunian Plains, is one of the historic places where the fate of our civilization hung in the balance in its struggle with the East. During many centuries, the vast plain, which ends at the foot of this high hill, exercised an irresistible attraction over the peoples of Asia. Along the road which they followed from the frontiers of China, it formed an admirable halting place where they could erect their tents for a while, let their horses breathe for a short space and, after watering them at the great river, once more resume their march towards the conquest and booty of the West. At the very foot of the hill of Buda, Attila established his camp, that celebrated Etzelburg, which, in the imagination of the poet of the Nibelungen, seemed to be the center of the world. After him many more hordes of Tartars or Mongolians disported themselves in that plain, appearing and disappearing like columns of dust, or like the mirages which the fairy Delibab delights to make appear on the horizon of those flat countries. Only the Hungarians, who came, it is said, from the region of the Pamirs, installed themselves firmly in the country. For a long time they were the terror of western Europe, until the day when, renouncing the worship of the White Stallion, they embraced the Roman religion and became the champions of Christianity against their brothers in Asia.

That happened a thousand years ago, in the reign of Saint Stephen the King. The hill of Buda was then still untenanted, for those war-like herdsmen cared only for vast pastures, where horses and sheep might graze peacefully, and which reminded them of the steppes from whence they came. But having been initiated by their new religion into the idea of life in cities, they climbed the hill and constructed on its summit, for the first time, churches, houses, and ramparts.

For centuries that fortified rock became the stake for which the East and West fought. From the far distant steppes, men with narrow eyes and yellow complexions came to attack it, and all feudal Europe rushed to its defense. Princes of the House of Anjou, grandnephews of Saint Louis, conducted a crusade here, at the same time bringing to Hungary the brilliant French civilization of the fourteenth century. From the Danube to the Adriatic, the country became covered with towns, castles, and monasteries. Here, on this very plateau, masons from Bray-sur-

Somme erected a royal castle which was exactly like the admirable mansions of the Ile de France. Every day the sacred kingdom of St. Stephen became more and more like a Western country; when suddenly a new horde appeared, even more formidable than the Huns of Attila or the Tartars of Batu-Khan. During more than half a century, two Transylvanian heroes, John Hunyadi and Mathias Corvin, resisted the attacks of the Turks. The Angelus which is rung at midday still commemorates the service which they rendered to Christianity four hundred years ago. Never did the hill of Buda appear more brilliant than in those days, when its very existence was in peril every moment. Latin civilization, which had originally conquered the hill by bringing to it first Christianity and then the spirit of the Anjous, blossomed anew, but this time under the semi-pagan form of the Renaissance. King Mathias summoned Italian artists around him, built palaces and churches, and filled them with precious objects and unique manuscripts, so that his rude fortress became a town after the fashion of the cities of Tuscany and Umbria. Great wagons, accompanied by armed escorts, brought to Buda cloth from Flanders, wines from the Rhine, and all the other products of Europe. Then, continuing on their way through the Saxon villages of Transylvania, towards Adrianople and the East, they returned from thence laden with spices, perfumes, carpets, and damascened arms. The merchants also made use of the Danube route; innumerable galleys, navigated by Turkish slaves, ascended and descended the river in order to exchange their merchandise with Venetian vessels laden with the riches to be found in Italy and in the ports of the Levant.

Then suddenly the catastrophe came. The Hungarian Army was annihilated by the Janissaries at Mohacs, and the citizens of Buda carried the keys of their city to the conquerors at the ancient Alba Royal, the tomb of the earliest kings of Hungary. Asia installed itself on the hill. Everything that recalled France or Italy was destroyed or taken away. King Mathias' cathedral became a mosque; Soliman's galleys carried off, in twelve hundred buffalo hide cases, all the treasures of the town; and for a long time afterwards one could see the statues of Hunyadi, of Mathias Corvin and his wife, and the great bronze sconces which ornamented the palace, exposed as trophies on the Hippodrome at Byzantium. Towns, castles, monasteries were destroyed, and the whole country was ravaged. Hungary became once more what she had been at the time of the first invasions: an immense expanse of pasturage and swamps. Two and a half centuries later, when Charles of Lorraine, at the head of an army to which all the nations of Europe had contributed soldiers, once more attacked the fortress, nothing remained of the monuments and treasures which the Anjous and Hunyadis had gathered together there.

During these last years, the Hungarians have tried to give back some splendor to this old city of Buda. Since the time when I used to stroll there, they have built ramparts and bastions, redoubts and turrets and gigantic staircases, reconstructed the Church of Mathias, and erected buildings in medieval style, in order to recall to the imagination the glory of olden days. But it is impossible to remake the past. Even by employing a great deal of science and a great deal of love, you cannot give life to that which has ceased to exist. What time has destroyed can only be resuscitated in the mind of a dreamer. It is an entirely German idea to solidify dreams and condense smoke. These pedantic reconstructions have always been in favor on the banks of the Rhine, where a romantic ruin is transformed into a pretentious new castle, and a crumbling ancient keep, haunted by the river fairies and the spirits of the air, into a ridiculous mass of masonry from which imagination and the night birds take wing so as to leave the place to the caretaker in possession. There, romantic melancholy is at once transformed into a rather foolish desire to give an aggressive material existence to things which are little more than a remembrance. In this desire to restore things that once existed, and to perpetuate the appearance of the past, there is more of vanity than of true poetry. Time, atmosphere, and the haze which envelopes the actual past are all suppressed in order to prove, in a clumsy fashion, that the power which built those crumbling walls long ago is still living and active. But these blocks of stone, gathered together with so much art, only display to us the embodiment of the cold dreams of architects and archaeologists; they can only afford us some illusion in the evening mist, and all this modern antiquity displeases where the ruins themselves enchanted us.

Yes, I find again today in Buda the Middle Ages of the Anjous and the Corvins, but it is quite new, aggressive, blinding alike to the spirit and the eye. On that height where the masons of Bray-sur-Somme and the Italian artists had given free play to their genius; the German spirit has only inspired a dull pupil's copy. How greatly do I prefer to all that heroic bric-a-brac the part of Buda which has preserved its character as a little bourgeois town, with its drowsy old streets and its old, simple yellow houses, which belong to a good period and do not attempt to impose upon you, but accept, with so modest a charm, the humble life which time has brought them! Beside their rusty wells, in their inner courtyards, I can catch the murmur that history makes around the old fortress far better than among all that false decoration in medieval style. The mass of stones, which tries so hard to be eloquent, only mars the harmony, whereas the simplest inscription on the plastered walls at once awakens our feeling, even as the slightest noise resounds in the silence of the night.

And here, in passing by, I recognized one of the pleasantest places in Buda, to which I often resorted in former days. It is a confectioner's shop, dating back to the Directorate or the first days of the empire. Nothing has been changed in the wainscots, chandeliers, mirrors, and pier glasses, or in the little Winged Victories that hold up crowns over the compôte dishes. The friezes, the moldings, and the whole decoration are just as they were when the first tenant took over the place and established his shop there. I entered and all was familiar to me; in the show cases still the thousand and one little articles made of paste and sugar, ridiculous inventions, in hopelessly old-fashioned taste, which seemed as if they also were a hundred years old.

It was there that I used to betake myself on certain foggy days when homesickness beset me and sip a curious liqueur that smelt like a chemist's shop.

A poor young Frenchman lost in that foreign town, and having, alas! no other amusement but that of dreaming of the past, I often heard the Angelus ringing at midday, which nowhere makes so lasting an impression on the human soul as on that high plateau where it rang out for the first time. There, also, I often saw in imagination the rider with the bloody sword whom in old days, in hours of peril, the kings of Buda used to send from castle to castle to call the whole nobility of Hungary to arms. And this morning as I sat in the silence of that little shop with the faded gilding, and mingling those dreams of a thousand years ago with the emotions and events of yesterday, I said to myself that perhaps after all they forgot too completely, on that recent day at the Trianon, the immense effort against Asia which this ancient fortress of the West had maintained during many centuries on behalf of the whole of the Christian world.

III

— THE HOUSE OF ORCZI —

The great flat town of Pest, which faces the hill of Buda on the opposite bank of the Danube, has not the same romantic and warlike history as the old fortress; but it too has suffered the formidable attacks of the East, attacks of a strange kind, invisible, many times repeated, in truth more resembling an inundation which rises imperceptibly than a great collision of armies of which grand historical pictures can be painted. The East, which was expelled two centuries ago from the fortress of Buda, cunningly introduced itself into the open town of Pest, and one fine day it was discovered to be master of the place.

This is how it happened.

At the beginning of the last century, Pest was a suburb of Buda, almost entirely inhabited by German merchants. These Germans, natives of Thuringia, of Franconia, or of Swabia, were the children of the serfs sent by the empress Maria Theresa, like a herd of human cattle, to colonize the country that had been depopulated by two hundred years of Ottoman occupation. They established their shops in those one-storied brick houses, with the long steep roofs, of which one or two examples still remain here and there in the town, but which are fast disappearing. These artisans or small tradesmen formed an honest, modest, and diligent population, and while still preserving their language they soon adapted themselves to the manners of the Hungarian people. Apart from a few Levantines, Greeks, and Armenians, and also a sprinkling of Austrians from Vienna, who held the larger business operations and the bank in their hands, these Germans had no serious competitors—from the earliest times the Magyars took no interest in commerce—and their affairs prospered. Suddenly, however, a figure appeared in the town who certainly was not unknown to them, but whose activity had until then been confined to the villages.

There have always been Jews in the Hungarian rural districts. Some came from Russia and some from Poland, where they teemed; some from Austria, where, before the Revolution of 1848, they could neither settle where they pleased nor, even if settled, had any right to found a home. Only the eldest son of a family was authorized to take a wife; as for the other children, they had the choice of celibacy, which was contrary to their religious law, or else of emigrating into a more liberal country. Very naturally a large number of them went into Hungary, where they found a rich country and a good-natured reception, very different from that which was usually their lot! Some entered the service of a seigneur in the capacity of Hazijido, that is to say of House Jew, steward, general utility man; others settled in the villages, generally as tavern keepers, and played about the same part with the villagers, as the Hazijido did with the noble layman or ecclesiastical dignitary. In the midst of a completely rural population, which despised everything that did not concern cattle breeding or the tilling of the soil, this stranger appeared as a being sent direct from God or the Devil, no one quite knew which, but as indispensable as the sun or the rain. It was a strange phenomenon: these people, who came no one knew whence, barely tolerated, without civil rights or any other protection than the goodwill of the seigneur or the good nature of the peasants, despised as vagabonds by the settled population of the country, cursed as the executioners of Christ by the Magyars, who were deeply attached to their Christian traditions, were yet able by sheer intellectual force to impose their domination on the whole rural life of the country.

At that time, it was easy for the great lords and the small landed nobility—the "gentry" as they are called, who are so numerous in Hungary—to live in the country in comfort and affluence. Labor cost nothing, and one lived in abundance on the products of the soil with no thought for the morrow. But in 1848, the abolition of serfdom changed all that. The small nobility suffered especially, for in order to give lands to the emancipated serfs, large inroads were made upon their properties, whereas the domains of the magnates and the great ecclesiastical seigneurs were left almost intact. The gentry received some compensation for these losses but paid in paper money which was rapidly discredited. So it happened that many of the smaller nobility, dispossessed of a part of their lands and finding it extremely difficult to cultivate the remainder now that they were forced to pay their people, flocked to Budapest, endeavoring to find posts in the administration which were practically sinecures, but which would still give them the illusion that they were in authority. What happened to their domains? The House Jews were still there! And as if by the decree of the Divine Will, the same revolution which abolished serfdom gave them the right, which they had never possessed before, of owning the land. They threw themselves greedily upon these properties, which their long feet had walked over for years without being able to acquire them for their own use.

Sometimes the owner could not bear the idea of parting with a property the name of which he bore. In order to continue the connection, he began by burying in it all that remained of his fortune; then he borrowed of his Jew, who ultimately turned him out of his own house. In other cases, the Hazijido rented the domain for nine years, and during those nine years he exploited the land intensively; an "exploitation by plunder," according to a recognized expression. Then, when the land had become exhausted and the buildings had fallen into disrepair, and when the renewal of the lease came to be in question, he demanded a reduction of rent on the ground that the land no longer produced what it used to do. The landowner then found himself in an awkward position. What was he to do? Should he give up his town life and that pleasant office in some ministry, where for eight hours every day he polished his nails, smoked Egyptian cigarettes, and talked politics while he jeered at the Jews? Should he give up the walks on the banks of the Danube which he enjoyed at midday and at five, when he strolled leisurely between a double row of idlers seated on benches beneath the thin acacia trees; should he say goodbye to his cafe and his club, to all those town pleasures in which he passed such an agreeable time while waiting for the moment to arrive when he should marry some rich young burgher's daughter, of course a converted Jewess? Should he put his estate in order? That would require money, and he had not a penny, or at least the little that remained to him was necessary in order to enable him to cut a figure in the world. Only one solution remained possible for him: he must sell his land to the Hazijido. That is what he decided to do.

As to the great nobles, even after serfdom was abolished, they continued to lead the same ostentatious lives as before in Vienna or in the other large towns of Europe. They mortgaged their domains, and becoming embarrassed for ready money, they demanded advances upon their rents from their Jews. At the death of the seigneur, the estate was found to be burdened with debt, and it was divided among several heirs, of whom some were always found who wished to sell their shares. The Jew was always there! How many of those Hazijido are today owners of the very houses where their ancestors arrived in days gone by, in their long black kaftans, cringing timorously with bent backs; and where they lived for so long, treated with contempt by even the least of the lackeys!

When the sons of those Jews had at last got their full plumage, by which I mean had accumulated some money in their pockets and a little instruction in their minds, they also took wing for Budapest. They, however, had no intention of burying themselves there under the waste paper of the administration; they were determined rather to throw themselves into those occupations which give real power.

The old-established Germans of Pest beheld the arrival of these intruders with horror. How was it possible that these men, unimaginative, bound up in routine, and honest as they were, should hold their own against these newcomers who dominated them by their energy, their wonderfully keen insight into business, and very often by an absolute absence of all scruples? One after another, the sons of these old-established merchants did, in their turn, what the sons of the gentry (whose character and ways, by living so closely with them, they had adopted) had already done. They forsook the pursuit of trade and embarked on the liberal careers disdained by the nobility. They became lawyers, doctors, and professors. Thus the banks, industrial undertakings, and all the high commerce of Pest fell into the hands of Israel.

In proportion as there, as elsewhere, money acquired an importance which it did not formerly possess, the old-established Jews of Hungary quitted the villages more and more in order to settle in the towns, where their genius adapted itself with marvelous facility to the new forms of financial and industrial activity. They alone, however, were not sufficiently numerous to suffice for all the needs of industry, commerce, and finance. The Magyars, indolent as they were, would have been led willy-nilly to participate in this movement of affairs, had there not existed on the frontiers of their country an immense Hebrew reservoir capable of furnishing an indefinite number of men wherever there was something to undertake or some gain to be realized. These Jews, who were called by their coreligionists themselves "wild Jews," came either straight from Galicia or arrived in Pest after having made a stay in the villages of Upper Hungary, just sufficiently long to enable them to amass a little hoard, enough to act as a nest-egg with which to make their fortunes.

It was these wild Jews who, supported and maintained by their wave-like inroads, again and again renewed that invasion of Pest which had been begun long ago by the older Jews of Hungary, who themselves had come from the same region. They continue to arrive daily. The place where one can best see them at the moment of arrival is a remarkable house, where I used often to go at all hours of the day. The place is well known; it is called the house of Orczi.

In the time of Maria Theresa, a Magnate, belonging to the great family of Orczi, caused to be constructed, in order to embellish Pest, a vast building, let out in flats, which was considered a marvel. It really united in itself all the elegancies of that epoch, great mansard roofs, baskets of flowers in wrought iron rising above the cornices, three enormous interior courts, surrounded by galleries on the first floor, vast carriage entrances large enough for traveling coaches drawn by four post horses to pass through. Soon, however, this beautiful house lost its elegant clients. A few rich, Jewish merchants installed themselves in the house, and heavy wagons, bringing bales of merchandise, passed through the great archways, instead of the traveling coaches of former days.

The Jew attracts the Jew. At Pest, which was a new town, there was no ghetto as at Pressburg, Vienna, Krakow, or Prague. Besides, the Jews are so accustomed to living tightly wedged against one another that even in prosperous times, even when they are at liberty to live where they will, they assemble together where they can feel each other's elbows pressing into their sides and breathe their own peculiar atmosphere. Accordingly, they spontaneously made a ghetto of the house of Orczi. And there, as in a ghetto, there was to be found a synagogue, with its complement of rabbis, its chanters, its beadles, its ritual butchers, its washers of corpses, its ritual baths for men and for women; and also a little cafe, which for a long time was the only stock exchange in Pest, before the creation of the edifice on the banks of the Danube. There business was discussed, prices were fixed; there the country proprietor met the Jew who bought his produce; there dreams of fortune were dreamed, which, by some inexplicable miracle or special divine privilege, were destined to be speedily transformed into positive realities for this elect race. That cafe was the arena of those agile spirits who transformed the small market town into the great city of today. It might have been said that it was the heart of Judaism in Pest, even had there been no synagogue over the cabaret. The cafe, the synagogue, the baths, and the ritual butcher's shop of the house of Orczi still exist today, but in the condition of a place through which fifty years of Jewish life have passed. Little by little, as the better-class Jews conquered the town, they abandoned the house where so many great fortunes had been built up. The old ghetto of the rich became the ghetto of the poor, the meeting place of all those Galician Jews who were still wild or hardly tamed and who daily arrived from Poland or from the Carpathians. There is one fleeting moment when one can still surprise them just as I used to see them in the high valleys of the Waag or in the Polish plain.

That is at dusk, at the Minchah hour of prayer. Mount to the synagogue, which is situated on the first floor, where the rite is celebrated as it is celebrated in Galicia according to the Hassidic ritual, with gesticulations and cries, and you will find them there, if I may so express it, in all their freshness. Many of them have not yet had the time or even the desire to change their costume, but the majority have already transformed themselves more or less. That crowd from the East, marching towards Europe, has already accomplished one stage. Among the round hats and the long, greasy frock coats, you find here and there a tall hat, a homburg, a shabby billycock, and a whole collection of cast-off waistcoats and coats from the old clothes shop. On many of the faces one now sees only a tress of hair on the temples, or a curl, or a sort of frizziness of fair hair or, as it were, a black comma, which mingles with the hair of the beard, instead of the long ringlets. That, however, which always remains intact, always unaltered in that synagogue, is something that survives all changes of costume and fortune among the children of Israel, and even superficial changes of thought; something religious, unanimous, enthusiastic, which here, despite its nauseating odor, is really fervent and powerful.

As I watched them gesticulating and vociferating their prayers, I asked myself often what could be the everyday occupations of these men, engaged in the mysteries of trade? Through what labyrinth of business combinations did all those bodies and all those minds struggle, that they might gain a few pence or enormous sums of money? To these questions I could return no answer, excepting that one thing would certainly happen: infallibly, this wild Jew, in his ancient costume, will in a few weeks become that weird mannequin whom the old clothes merchant has dressed up in his wares. That mannequin, in his turn, will take on the quasi-bourgeois air of the stout personage whom I see on the almemar, and who appears as it were disguised in his tall hat and with gold-rimmed glasses on his nose. That stout man will eventually leave this synagogue (which is really too redolent of his native Poland) for the synagogue at Pest, that enormous new building in one of the handsomest quarters of the town, where people no longer vociferate or gesticulate, and where the lean, wild Jew seems to have miraculously become, as if by the touch of Aaron's rod, fat, overfed, obese, correct, and well dressed.

In less than fifty years those people of the house of Orczi have transformed Budapest. They have made an enormous capital out of the small, rural, bourgeois city of former days, which may not please, for all styles are jumbled together in a horrible discord of iron, brick, and reinforced cement, but to which one must allow some measure of smartness and power. Such rapid development and so fine an outward show flattered the Magyar spirit, always prone to be attracted by pomp and grandeur. They were grateful to these newcomers, who forced them, so to say, into a larger world, and who, in addition, brought practical intelligence and activity into their affairs, in which qualities they themselves were singularly wanting. Moreover, their naturally generous spirit was glad to receive liberally these Orientals, who usually were badly treated by their neighbors. At most they only allowed themselves toward the Jews the same slight air of disdain or of superiority with which they treated the Romanian, the Serb, the German, the Slovak, or any other member of an alien race whom they received into their country. The Jews, on their side, happy to find a hospitality in Hungary which opened to them so easy an entrance to the nations of the West, endeavored to become more Hungarian than the Hungarians themselves. They adopted their language, their manners, their sentiments, even their patriotism, with that excessive ardor which is so characteristic of their race. Many of them, indeed, were sincere. How was it possible not to be grateful to a country which had received them so lavishly and where they enjoyed a position unknown to them in any other place in the world?

But this good understanding between Jews and Magyars was only an appearance, favored by the ability of one side and the illusionist spirit of the other. Under this pompous facade, as under the plaster and sham marble of the houses, there was only brick and rubble—misunderstanding and hatred. This at once became evident when misfortune fell upon Hungary, and when a social tragedy was enacted at Budapest, the prologue to which was the murder of Count Tisza.

IV

— THE MURDER OF COUNT TISZA —

The Tiszas do not belong to the great Magyar nobility; they were hardly ever seen at Court and their activities would not have spread beyond the limits of their province had it not been that by reason of their old-established position as ardent Calvinists they had always played a part in the General Synods of Hungary. In 1848, when the Hungarians, at the call of Kossuth, rose against Austria, three brothers of the house of Tisza took service in the Army of Independence. One of them, left for dead on the field of battle, only survived his fifty wounds by a miracle. He was "the man with the heart of stone," the hero of a celebrated novel in which Maurus Jokai glorified the small provincial nobility, who were divided between hatred of the Hapsburgs and natural aversion to the new order of things so fatal to their privileges, and who finally chose the side of the revolution, contrary to their own interests.

The youngest of the three Tiszas long remained faithful to the ideas for which he had fought, sword in hand. When he was elected to the Hungarian Parliament, however, he gradually became subject to the influences which acted so powerfully on the spirit of the Hungarian nobles once they had left their provinces. At home, absorbed in their little local life, they did not realize the strength which Hungary drew from her union with Austria. They grasped it much more when they went to Budapest or Vienna. Also, it was hard for them to resist the seductions of a court which had remained so imposing and was at the same time prodigiously clever in flattering those who might be of use to it.

The former comrade in arms of Kossuth rallied to the compromise of 1867, which assured internal liberty to Hungary but subordinated her to Austria in all questions concerning the army and foreign policy. He became prime minister and remained so till his death. It seemed quite natural that his son Stephen should take his place, for the emperor Franz Joseph loved the Tisza family and detested having new names and new faces about his person. For thirty years Stephen Tisza directed the affairs of his country. Physically, he was a tall, thin man, hard featured, with a piercing glance behind his big, round spectacles, his hair brushed back, a fine forehead, thin lips, and an uneven beard which he trimmed with scissors. In the photograph which I have before me, and which depicts him as I saw him for a moment not long ago at an official ceremony, he is dressed in a gala costume made of satin, silk, and fur, a cap with an aigrette in it on his head, a Turkish scimitar at his side, and a furred tippet fastened over the shoulder with a chain of gold and precious stones. In ordinary life, however, he was quite different. He wore elastic-sided boots and a tall hat which had seen hard service; usually he was clad in an old frock coat whose military cut gave him something of the air of an officer on half-pay. Notwithstanding that he so disdained the fashions of the day, he was an accomplished sportsman and a first-rate man with the foils, who, even when he was president of the council, accepted all challenges and generally wounded his adversary. He was a keen rider and devoted to hunting and to long rides over his property, and up to the end of his life, although he was long past fifty, he rode every year in the races.

Morally, his was a strong soul, simple, equable, dominated by big sentiments which were almost elemental. Obstinate in thought, very austere and inclined to self-sacrifice, he seemed to find a morose pleasure in the unpopularity in which he always lived, although he did not possess, in the smallest degree, that contempt of humanity which is so often engendered in a politician by the experience of parliamentary life. He had a taste for friendship and demanded character and fidelity from his friends rather than proofs of great talent. Though devoid of arrogance and without a trace of vanity, he clung tenaciously to the privileges of the nobility, which are still so considerable in Hungary. In short, he was a vigorous personality who combined the rigidity of a Calvinist with the sentiments of a great seigneurial landowner and with the Hungarian pride of race. He bore, indeed, a great resemblance (though he was more scrupulous and of a nobler moral fiber) to the man in the big hat, whose picture on the wall had become an obsession to me in former days.

It was not an easy task to conduct the affairs of Hungary. The Magyars, so proud of their domination over the Serbs, the Romanians, and the Croats, all those diverse peoples whom ten centuries of life in common had united in Hungary, without in any way succeeding in blending them, had in their turn been forced to submit to a kind of vassalage which they only accepted with resentment. Their exasperated pride constantly urged them to break the ties which bound them to Austria; but the instinct of self-preservation warned them that without the support of the hated Austrians they would be at the mercy of all the alien races that struggled for freedom within their boundaries. Hence there arose a secret fever which, despite all compromises, was never appeased.

That fever recurred every year when it was a question of voting the credits for the combined army of the Dual Monarchy; and scenes of disgraceful violence took place in the Hungarian Parliament. In that army, of which the Magyars rightly considered they formed the most solid element, they desired that their national contingent should have its special flag and that the word of command should be given in Hungarian, and not in German. Vienna, however, would not hear of this. Count Tisza, placed in the dilemma of either displeasing his compatriots or of weakening the army by breaking its unity, did not hesitate to employ force in order to get the credits voted.

With the same inflexible obstinacy, he would alter nothing in the system of limited suffrage which maintained in his country a really feudal regime, to which he was passionately attached with all the depth of his nature. Above all, he realized that with an enlarged suffrage the Magyars would soon cease to have the mastery in a state where they had always been outnumbered. His uncompromising policy irritated and aroused indignation; his obstinacy in maintaining himself in power was considered to be tyrannical. But he continued to impose his will on Parliament without ever yielding on any point. Hungary recognized and detested in this self-opinionated man the ill-balanced destiny which was the outcome of her history, but in the end she submitted to him even as she submitted to her fate.

When the war broke out, no one had any doubt that Count Tisza had worked resolutely to hasten on the conflict. Had he not always upheld, in the Chamber, the views of the Austrian general staff? His admiration for Bismarck, his devotion to Germany, was not a secret to anyone; and the emperor William was wont to say that the prime minister of Hungary was the most able man in the Dual Monarchy. Franz Joseph had more confidence in him than he had shown towards any other person in the course of his long reign. Would he have passed over the advice of his minister if Tisza had pleaded for a peaceful solution?

Besides, no questions of the kind were raised: it seemed so obvious that, during the tragic hours of July 1914, Count Tisza had assumed the whole responsibility for the war. In Austria, as in Hungary, he was given the sole credit for it. The flattered vanity of the Magyars loudly acclaimed their prime minister, the man who had held the fate of Europe in his hands at a decisive moment in her history. The animosity which had always surrounded that intractable individual suddenly gave place to an immense popularity.

Once more there was misunderstanding between Tisza and his country. Tisza did not want war; but that was a secret which he could tell to no one. He did not even divulge it at the moment when his doing so might have turned aside the weapons of his murderers. The tragedy of his fate lies less in his tragic assassination than in the high moral beauty of the conscientious scruple which prevented him from speaking.

Count Tisza's secret has been made known to us since then by the publication of what passed at the Imperial Council held at Vienna on July 7th, 1914, under the presidency of Count Berchtold, Minister for Foreign Affairs and of the Imperial Household.[1]

It was only a few days after the assassination of the archduke Franz Ferdinand at Sarajevo. There were present at this conference Count Stürgkh, president of the Austrian Council; Count Tisza, president of the Hungarian Council; the Chevalier de Bilinski, minister of dual finance; the Chevalier Krobatin, minister of war; Baron Conrad de Hoetzendorf, chief of the general staff; Rear Admiral de Kailer, representing the minister of marine; and finally Count Hoyos, secretary of embassy, who drew up the minutes. Count Berchtold opened the conference by declaring that his object was to consider whether, after the assassination of the heir to the throne, the moment had not come to render Serbia forever innocuous. He was armed with the assurance that the emperor William and the chancellor Bethmann would support Austria unre-

---

[1] Diplomatic papers concerning the events which preceded the war of 1914 published by the Ministry for Foreign Affairs of the Austrian Republic.

servedly, and he agreed with Berlin that it would be better to take action unknown to Italy or Romania in order to prevent blackmail. There could hardly be a doubt of Russia's intervention, for the whole tendency of her policy was to endeavor to unite the Balkan nations (including Romania) in order to let them loose at an opportune moment upon the Dual Monarchy. It would also be advisable to act quickly so as to arrest, by a prompt settling of accounts with Serbia, that Balkan push which would become irresistible if they waited longer.

Tisza was aware of Berchtold's ideas, for he had heard them expressed by the count a few days previously, and he had been so deeply moved by them that he had written on the same day to the emperor Franz Joseph that to take that view of the matter would, in his opinion, be to commit a fatal error, and one for which he would in no wise be prepared to share the responsibility. Speaking in his turn, he recognized that the latest revelations regarding the murder of the archduke and the insolence of the Belgrade press had brought an eventual war with Serbia nearer than he had imagined on the day after the attempt. But he declared that he would never give his consent to the most regrettable project of an attack to be launched suddenly against Serbia without giving her warning, such as it seemed they were even now contemplating and plotting with Berlin to carry out. It would be bringing Austria-Hungary into bad odor with Europe and would draw down upon her the hostility of the whole Balkan Peninsula, with the exception of the Bulgarians, who were too weak at this moment to give any efficient support. In his opinion, therefore, it would be necessary to put forward clearly what was demanded of Serbia and only present an ultimatum to her if she refused the demands formulated in a preliminary note. These demands should be severe, but at the same time not such as Serbia could not possibly accept. If Serbia submitted to them, the Vienna cabinet would have carried off a diplomatic success which would heighten the prestige of the Dual Monarchy among all the Balkan states; if she did not submit, then the count agreed there could only be a war-like solution to the conflict. But even in the latter event, he drew attention then and there to the fact that any war-like measures must aim at a simple diminution of Serbian territory and not at her complete annihilation; firstly, because Russia would fight to the death to prevent it, and secondly, because he, as prime minister of Hungary, would oppose all annexation of new territory.

In order to understand the reasons which made Tisza speak in this way, it is necessary to know that the tragic end of the archduke Franz Ferdinand, while it filled him with horror, had at the same time relieved him from an anxiety which had long oppressed him. He had always contemplated the moment when the archduke would succeed to the old emperor-king with deep misgiving. The archduke detested the Magyars as a race which centuries of efforts had never been able to subjugate to the absolutism of the Hapsburgs. He was credited with the intention of augmenting the Slav influence in the monarchy to the detriment of that of the Hungarians, and several indications gave reason to suppose that he would hold cheap the liberties which Hungary had so painfully wrung from the despotism of Vienna. These supposed sentiments of the archduke were rather guessed at than positively known, for that enigmatical person never betrayed his thoughts. All that could be extracted from his disquieting personality consisted of a few quick flashes which half revealed a fanatic temperament and sudden outbursts which did not even spare the emperor. His disingenuous or brutal criticism of political methods which he considered superannuated, his evident haste to conduct his uncle to the grave, and many details which escaped ordinary eyes, but which his post at court and his almost familiar relations with Franz Joseph made known to Tisza, all contributed to feed the latter's anxiety. He knew, also, that Ferdinand nursed a tenacious hatred towards him, as everything in his personality could not but be displeasing: the authority which he enjoyed in his country, his uncourtier-like spirit, his inflexible will, even his religion. The archduke, a pupil of the Innsbruck Jesuits, held Calvinism in especial abhorrence.

The murder of the heir to the Austro-Hungarian throne was not calculated therefore to arouse much resentment against Serbia in Tisza's breast. Besides, he only saw inconvenience in any annexation of territory which, by augmenting the already excessive number of Slavs in the Dual Monarchy, could only in his opinion further reduce the Magyar preponderance.

He went on to say that it was not for Germany to decide whether the hour had come for Vienna to make war upon Serbia. For his part, he considered the moment an unfavorable one. It was likely that the Romanians, too, would be against them, for they were showing themselves very hostile to the Magyars at that time. It would be necessary to maintain large forces in Transylvania in order to. intimidate them. On the other hand, by patiently awaiting the result of the efforts which Germany was so auspiciously making to attract Bulgaria into the circle of the Triple Alliance, Romania and Serbia might soon be isolated, and the Romanians would then return to the Triple Alliance of their own accord. Finally, the longer war was delayed, the more the balance of power between France and Germany would lean towards the latter, in view of the low birth rate in France, and the more troops would be available in Germany to oppose Russia. For these various reasons it seemed to him that a warlike solution would be unreasonable; he thought it would be wiser to inflict a diplomatic defeat upon Serbia, which would open the way for the pursuit of an efficacious policy in the Balkans.

Count Berchtold replied that diplomatic successes had never hitherto led to anything but short periods of amelioration in their relations with Belgrade, and that only an energetic attack could put an end to the efforts of the partisans of a greater Serbia, which were felt as far as Agram and Zara. As to the Romanians, he considered that they were less to be feared now than in the future because the ties between them and Serbia could only grow closer. It was quite true that King Carol had recently expressed to the emperor Franz Joseph doubts as to the manner in which he could perform his duty as an ally, for he had to take into consideration the sentiments of his subjects, but it was hardly conceivable that he would allow himself to be dragged into a war against the monarchy. The Bulgarian menace would also be a cause of restraint upon him.

Finally, Count Tisza's remark concerning the proportion of forces between France and Germany seemed to him hardly convincing, taking into consideration the extraordinary development of the Russian population, which more than made up for the lowness of the French birth rate.

After Berchtold's reply to the Hungarian prime minister, Count Stürgkh, the Austrian prime minister, declared that to him also war appeared to be necessary. He agreed fully with Count Tisza that the monarchy was not to take orders from Germany as to whether or not it was to begin hostilities, but at the same time it was necessary to consider carefully whether, if proofs of weakness were given today, Germany might not later on be found less willing than she was now to give her support without reserve. As for the manner in which it would be suitable to enter upon the war, that was a question of detail. If the council rejected all idea of a sudden attack upon Serbia, it would be well to seek another way by which to arrive at the same end.

The Chevalier de Bilinski, minister of finance in the Dual Monarchy, observed that according to the view of General Potiorek, governor of Bosnia and Herzegovina, who had followed the Pan-Serbian agitation for two years on the spot, it would be impossible to hold that territory unless Belgrade were finished with once for all. To imagine, as Count Tisza did, that it was possible to be satisfied with a mere diplomatic success was to fail to realize the excitement which reigned in Bosnia, where it was openly said among the people that King Peter of Serbia would soon come to deliver the country. To his mind, the Serbs were only amenable to force, and to humiliate King Peter would only result in still further irritating the Serbian mind and would definitely do more harm than good.

Count Tisza replied that he had the highest opinion of General Potiorek's military talents, but that he was obliged to point out that the Bosnian administration was not worth much; the police especially had cut a wretched figure in the affair of Sarajevo.[2] They had allowed six or seven individuals to remain on the route which the archduke was to traverse, although it was well known they were armed with revolvers and bombs. He could not see why the situation in Bosnia could not be improved by good police measures and administration.

Count Krobatin, minister of war, then spoke. His opinion naturally was that a diplomatic success would certainly be useless, and that from the military point of view it would be much better to make war at once rather than put it off till later because in the future the balance of power would perhaps no longer be in favor of the Dual Monarchy. Considering that the two last wars (the Russo-Japanese War and the Balkan War) had been begun without any preliminary declaration, he offered the advice that mobilization should be undertaken secretly, and that an ultimatum should only be sent when the mobilization was an accomplished fact, which would have the advantage—suppose Russia took part in the war—of placing the Austro-Hungarian Army in an excellent position, as it was well known that the Russian frontier corps were far from being up to their full complement on account of the harvest fur-

---

[2] The same General Potiorek who at the beginning of the war was so completely beaten by the Serbians.

loughs. A long discussion as to the aims and objects of the war then took place, the details of which do not appear in the minutes. Count Tisza's wish that, out of consideration for Russia, the Kingdom of Serbia should be diminished but not annihilated, was discussed. Count Stürgkh suggested that it would be best to overthrow the Kara-Georgevitch dynasty in order to give the crown to some European prince and to make the diminished Serbia a dependency of the Dual Monarchy. Once more Count Tisza drew the attention of his colleagues to the calamities that a European war would entail. He pressed them to take into consideration certain eventualities that might arise in the future, for example: Asiatic complications which might distract Russia from the interest she took in the Balkans, or a war of revenge undertaken by the Bulgarians against the Serbs, etc., any of which eventualities would improve the present situation.

Berchtold replied that it was indeed possible to conceive this or that happy conjunction of affairs, but it was necessary to realize the fact that the enemy were preparing a fight to the death, and that Romania was supporting the Russian and French diplomacy. Romania would not be won over until the Serbians were destroyed. Then only would Romania realize, isolated as she would be in the Balkans, that the Triple Alliance was her only support. As to believing that the Bulgarians could enter upon a war of revenge against Belgrade, that was a mere supposition, for Germany would only accept the idea of launching them upon the Serbs on the express condition that they should not attack the Romanians.

The minutes go on to say that the discussion continued for a long time before arriving at the conclusion that, as everyone except the president of the Hungarian Council held, a purely diplomatic success, even if it produced a complete humiliation of Serbia, would lead to nothing, and that it was necessary in consequence to present such terms to Serbia as would make her refusal a foregone conclusion, thus paving the way for a radical solution by force of arms.

Count Tisza continued his hand-to-hand fight and begged they would take note that, in his desire to draw as closely as possible to the other members of the council, he was ready to concede that the conditions offered to Serbia should be made very hard, but that he could not admit of their being made totally unacceptable. He demanded that the text of the note should be closely scrutinized, and that he should be informed of it before it was dispatched, stating that if his point of view was not sufficiently taken into consideration he should feel obliged to draw such personal conclusions as he should judge necessary.

The Council reassembled on the afternoon of the same day. The chief of the General Staff, Conrad de Hoetzendorf, gave explanations of a secret character on various military questions and on the probable course of a European war. These were not reported in the minutes.

As a conclusion to this debate, Count Tisza asked the council once more to weigh well their decision before embarking on the war. Then the points which were to appear in the note to the government at Belgrade were tentatively discussed. An understanding was not arrived at, but Count Berchtold remarked that even if there still remained a divergence between the point of view of the members of the council and Count Tisza, they had drawn closer together, for the proposals put forward by the president of the Hungarian Parliament would also undoubtedly lead to that settlement of accounts by war, which the other members present considered indispensable. But this interpretation of his point of view evidently did not satisfy Tisza, as he begged Count Berchtold, who was leaving for Ischl to rejoin the emperor, to hand to His Majesty a letter in which he would set forth his views on the situation.

The same evening, he returned to Budapest, and on the following day, July 8th, he received a telegram which Berchtold had sent hoping to influence him.

In this telegram, Berchtold told him that M. Tschirschky, the German ambassador at Vienna, had let him know that some decisive action against the Serbs on the part of Austria-Hungary was expected in Berlin: that in Germany it was not considered possible that the cabinet in Vienna should let slip such an opportunity; that the emperor William had written personally to King Carol to persuade Romania to remain neutral in the conflict; and that, if Vienna did not now take action, everyone in Germany would consider it a sign of regrettable weakness. That telegram did not alter Count Tisza's views. Directly he received it, he wrote the letter to the emperor which he had already announced. He first of all discussed in it the different possibilities which might produce a new situation that would be less favorable to Serbia and more advantageous to Austria. He then continued as follows:

When, after a careful study of the political situation, I think of the complete economic and financial upheaval, of the suffering and sacrifices which war would inevitably bring in its train, and after the most painstaking and conscientious consideration, I find I cannot face the idea of having any part in the responsibility for the proposed military attack upon Serbia. Far be it from me to propose a policy devoid of energy in regard to our neighbors. We cannot remain inert spectators of the agitation which results in exciting our own people against us and in fomenting crime. Not only the Serbian press and the official journals, but also the representatives of Serbia abroad, show so much hatred and are so wanting in the observance of international courtesy towards us, that our prestige on the one hand and our security on the other call imperatively for energetic action against Serbia. I am certainly not prepared to accept meekly all their provocations, and I am ready to accept the responsibility for a war which might result from their refusing our just demands. We must, however, leave to Serbia the possibility of avoiding a conflict at the price of a deep humiliation. We must be able to prove to the universe that if we entered upon the war, it was only in legitimate self-defense. My advice, therefore, is that we should address a note to Serbia couched in measured and non-menacing terms, in which we should set forward clearly our grievances and our demands. If the reply does not satisfy us, or if it is unduly delayed, we should then forward an ultimatum, and, if that also failed, commence hostilities. In that case we should find ourselves faced with a war that had been imposed upon us, a war such at is it is the duty of every nation to prosecute vigorously if it wishes to remain a state, and for which the responsibility would recoil upon our adversary, who would have let it loose by the refusal to behave as an honest neighbor even after the atrocious crime at Sarajevo. By acting in this manner, we would strengthen the chances of success of the German action at Bucharest, and it is even possible that Russia might abstain from taking part in the war. All appearances point to England exercising a soothing influence on the other Entente powers. There is no doubt, also, that the czar would reflect that it was hardly possible for him to take upon himself the role of defending anarchists and the assassins of kings.

I would add that in order to prevent complications with Italy and to assure ourselves of the sympathy of England, and above all to make it possible for Russia to remain a simple spectator of the war, we ought also, at an opportune moment and in a suitable form, to declare expressly that we had no intention of destroying Serbia and still less of annexing the country. In my opinion, I consider that at the conclusion of a war ending victoriously for us, the kingdom of

Serbia should be deprived, in favor of Greece, Albania, and Bulgaria, of the territories which she gained in the last Balkan war. For our own part, we ought to content ourselves with demanding the rectification of certain important strategic points on our frontier. Perhaps we could also demand a war indemnity, which would have the advantage of giving us the whip hand of Serbia for many years. These would appear to me to be the most suitable solutions if we make war. If, however, Serbia yields to our demands, we ought of course to accept her submission in good faith and not bar her retreat. We ought to content ourselves with humiliating her pride, and having won a diplomatic victory we would be able to pursue an advantageous policy in Bulgaria and in the other Balkan states. Such is the humble opinion which I have the honor to submit to your Majesty; I am deeply sensible of the grave responsibilities which rest in these critical times upon all persons whom your Majesty honors with his confidence. That responsibility is equally great whether we decide to act or to abstain from acting. I have well considered the matter and I have the honor to recommend an exactly middle course as indicated in the above memorandum. It appears to me not to put aside the possibility of a peaceful solution and to better our military position in many ways should war, after all, become inevitable. For myself, I have the honor to state, with the very greatest respect, that despite my devotion to your Majesty, or rather on account of that very devotion, it would be impossible for me to accept the solution of war at any price.

Evidently Franz Joseph was not convinced by Tisza's arguments, for on his return from Ischl Count Berchtold showed himself to be more than ever in favor of a violent policy. Germany, moreover, never ceased its pressure on the Vienna Cabinet. On July 12th, Count Szogeny, the Austro-Hungarian ambassador at Berlin, telegraphed to Count Berchtold that the kaiser and other competent authorities were eager for action to be taken against Serbia and charged him to assure Vienna that England would remain neutral. On July 14th, William II wrote the following involved letter to Franz Joseph, which, though hidden under a cloud of tender words, contained a most artful invitation to make war:

> My dear friend, I experience a feeling of real gratitude in noting that, at this time, when events of a tragic character have crowded upon you, which demand of you grave decisions, your thoughts should have turned to our friendship, and that you should have concluded your letter by renewing your assurance of it to me. I see in that close affection, which I consider a precious legacy transmitted to me by my grandfather and my father, and in the way in which you return it, the best guarantee for the protection of our countries. My respectful attachment to your person will allow you to measure how exceedingly painful it was to me to be forced to give up my journey to Vienna and to renounce that public manifestation of the lively share I take in your grief.[3]
>
> Your ambassador, an experienced man whom I sincerely esteem, will have transmitted to you my assurance that in all critical moments you will ever find me faithfully at your side, myself and my empire. A long-tried affection and our mutual obligations as allies demand this. It is a joyful duty for me to repeat it in this letter.
>
> The horrible crime at Sarajevo has brought to the light of day the malevolent maneuvers of demented fanatics and the Pan-Slavist plots which menace the

---

[3] The kaiser was to have come to Vienna for the obsequies of Franz Ferdinand.

safety of the state. I must abstain from taking up a definite position in the question which has arisen between your government and Serbia. I consider that it is not only the moral duty of all civilized countries, but also vital to their own continued existence, that they should oppose the most energetic measures to this propaganda of action, the principal object of which is to break the solid cohesion of monarchies. Nor am I blind to the serious dangers by which your states, and therefore the Triple Alliance, are menaced in consequence of the Russian and Serbian Pan-Slavist agitations, and I recognize the necessity for freeing the southern frontiers of your empire from this severe pressure.

I am therefore ready to second, as far as possible, the efforts of your government to prevent the formation of a new Balkan Alliance under the patronage of Russia, which would be directed against you, and at the same time to use my best endeavors to secure the adhesion of Bulgaria to the Triple Alliance in order to counteract this danger. In consequence of this, and despite certain hesitations to which the small reliance one can place on the Bulgarian character gives rise, I have given my envoy at Sofia the necessary instructions so that he may support the steps taken by your representative when he desires him to do so. Besides this, I have given orders to my Chargé d'Affaires at Bucharest to talk to King Carol in accordance with your indications, and by calling his attention to the new situation created by the late events in Serbia to impress upon him the necessity of detaching himself from Serbia and of restraining the agitation directed against your states. I have also at the same time insisted on the great importance that I attach to the continuance of the good understanding and confident alliance hitherto maintained with Romania. This good understanding should remain unimpaired even in the event of Bulgaria joining the Triple Alliance. In conclusion let me express the cordial wish that you may be able to find relaxation after these trying days during your stay at Ischl.

Pray, always believe in the sincere attachment and affection of your faithful friend William.

Thus the kaiser and the emperor Franz Joseph, their ministers, their military advisers, and everyone else urged towards war. What could Count Tisza do against such a powerful coalition? Should he send in his resignation? But if he did that, would he not be disobeying the aged sovereign whom he loved; would he not be repudiating the alliance with Germany, and would he not really be betraying his country? What chance would such a decision have of averting the catastrophe? Its only effect would be to diminish his people's faith in the justice of their cause and to create doubts and crises and internal complications at a moment when unity was so absolutely necessary. It might have been different if Tisza had felt that his country would support him. But all Hungary was carried away by its age-long hatred of the Slavs and was also clamoring for war. He himself did not reject the idea of war if Serbia, by a course of extreme insolence, rendered it inevitable. Finally, if Hungary remained a spectator of the conflict, who would guarantee that she would emerge safe and sound from the general war which was infallibly about to break out? Would she not be attacked alike by her enemies of old standing and by her allies of yesterday?

It was for these reasons and perhaps for others which have escaped me that Count Tisza, at the last Imperial Council, which was held on the July 19th, finally consented to the dispatch of the brutal ultimatum which was to result in war and which he had so long contested. He insisted once more that the council should make a public declaration to the effect that the monarchy was not seeking to annex any new territory. Even this was denied him.

One by one he had lost all the points of the game.

On the evening of the declaration of war, an immense crowd cheered him from the street under his windows. For the first time in his political life the nation seemed to be in agreement with him. What were his thoughts then? He remained silent. He accepted this sudden popularity, these acclamations, the mistaken homage which glorified in him ideas and resolutions which were not his. But one evening, when he returned to his home in the country, he said one word which showed what his real thoughts were. As the young woman who told me the story was congratulating him on all the flowers with which his carriage was piled up, he replied with a sad face: "If only these are not one day changed into stones."

Hungary was in danger from the very first months of the war. After their successes in Galicia, considerable masses of Russians tried to force the Carpathians. Then a terrible struggle began in that chaos of ice and rocks and forests, against the elements and man, and also against that scourge of God which is unknown to us, that death which strikes everywhere, which is overwhelming and ignoble—death by typhus. Troops from all the members of the Triple Alliance were successively sent to this front, but they were quickly exhausted, and it was necessary to recall them to less trying sectors. The Hungarians alone held on tenaciously in those heights. One must recognize that it was their endurance which barred the march of the Russian troops and for a long time turned the scale in the fortunes of war in favor of the Germans.

During that tragic time, Tisza behaved just as one would have expected. The energy which he displayed could only strengthen the idea that he was primarily responsible for this war, which he supported with his habitual firmness. The people who formed his entourage and who saw him daily at this time have told me that he never communicated the feelings which were agitating him to anyone; but his somber moods, the deepening lines in his face, revealed the profound torments of his soul to those about him. Even at times when events appeared to take a more favorable turn and seemed to presage success, he hardly seemed relieved. In the midst of the ever-growing difficulties, he maintained his marvelous power of work, his obstinate will, and that activity which had its eyes everywhere and spared no one, not even the high command.

Little by little we shall learn more precisely what were Count Tisza's relations with Germany during those terrible years, but even now we can catch glimpses which show us that they were not without storms. For instance, in 1915, when Germany was trying to prevent Romania from declaring in favor of the Allies, the kaiser suggested to Budapest the idea of giving up a part of Transylvania to the Romanians. Tisza replied that Hungary was fighting for the integrity of her territory and if it were necessary that sacrifices should be made to bring about peace, it was for Germany to make them.

In January 1917, he went to Berlin in order to combat the project of relentless submarine warfare. Baron Ghillany, minister for agriculture, who accompanied him on this journey, told me that at one moment the German authorities seemed shaken by his arguments. Count Tisza's opinion was transmitted to the emperor. The kaiser sent him word by the secretary of state, Zimmermann, that in any case the entry of the United States into the war was certain, whether there was or was not a new motive for their so doing. All the satisfaction that Tisza could obtain was an empty promise that Germany would seize the first opportunity of making an honorable peace, even at the price of a cession of territory.[4] This obstinate man was no more liked at Vienna than in Berlin, and the death of Franz Joseph took away the only support left him at the court. Up to his last moments, the old sovereign had never ceased to give him his confidence, and even to bestow upon him

---

[4] This testimony of Baron Ghillany is entirely confirmed by the debates on the Helfferich lawsuit.

marks of paternal affection, though he was the last man in the world to give way to effusive sentiments. On his side, Tisza was deeply attached to the emperor, and when he spoke of "the Master" it was always in terms which praised his high-bred manner, his ardor for work, his wonderful memory, and the wisdom which it is to be regretted that the old man did not vindicate by following the counsels of his minister in the month of July 1914!

The new emperor's first step was to dismiss the personnel that had grown old with his uncle. It soon became evident that Tisza would also be sacrificed. Was Tisza aware of this, or did his contempt for intrigues prevent him from having any suspicion of the plots which were being hatched against him? He never showed that he felt any distrust of his new master. The blow fell upon him with rude suddenness.

Whether the emperor Charles wanted to acquire popularity, whether he had taken up the old idea of the Hapsburgs of increasing the Slav influence in the monarchy to the detriment of the Hungarians, or whether he saw in this procedure simply the means of getting rid of his minister, we do not know, but the fact remains that he resolved to establish universal suffrage in Hungary. After two days of discussion, he ended by agreeing with Tisza on a plan for reforming the electorate. When, however, the final text of this agreement was submitted to the prime minister, he noticed with surprise that it did not correspond with the project previously agreed upon. He drew the emperor's attention to this. The emperor, who was leaving for the country, gave him an audience in his railway carriage, and without any explanation notified to Tisza that he was dismissed. What consequences did that abrupt action have upon the events which followed? What would have been Tisza's role in the attempts which the emperor Charles made towards a separate peace? Would he have rejected them as treasonable towards Germany, or would he have considered that the alliance ought to be sacrificed to the interests of the Dual Monarchy? Opinions differ on this point. After all, it is entirely an academic question. At the moment when the emperor made his famous attempt, Tisza was far from the court. He had rejoined his regiment of the Hussars of Debrecen, in which he had done his military service, as their colonel. They were now in the Carpathian Mountains, where he lived the life of the soldiers, sharing their sufferings and their rations, always at the most exposed post, and only leaving the army at rare intervals to perform his parliamentary duties.

He was at Budapest when the news arrived that General Franchet d'Esperey had broken through the Bulgarian front. The Germans were retreating in France, the Austrians were giving way on the Piave: Hungary was lost. As the catastrophe became more certain, a movement of deep hatred arose against Tisza. All the fury and rancor which a disastrous war could arouse was accumulated on Tisza's head. He was required to render an account for the misfortune into which he had plunged his country.

A less strong soul than his would have sought to defend itself by showing proofs that in July 1914 it was due to no remissness on his part that war had not been avoided. But at that time his friends and political partisans had noisily acclaimed him as the prime author of the conflict. He had not contradicted them, as he did not want to disturb public opinion, and consequently he had enjoyed immense popularity. Now that things were turning out badly, could he break the silence which he had so obstinately kept when it favored his reputation? Could he reveal his secret so as once more to derive a prodigious advantage from it, and so save his personal prestige in the general cataclysm?

In the sitting of the Hungarian Chamber on October 17th, which was without doubt the most moving of any which the old Parliament of Hungary had held, Tisza's last speech was calculated to raise the courage of the members and reinstate him in the good opinion of his country: "We have lost the war," he said, "but in this formidable fight the Hungarian nation has done everything to gain the esteem and respect of its enemies. The whole world can judge how our soldiers have tended the enemy's wounded and how our authorities have treated the strangers who remained within our boundaries. What nation has fought more heroically or with greater chivalry? A people does not exist that has fought for its existence so nobly and with so little hatred at heart as the Hungarians."

But nobody would listen any longer to the voice of this execrated man. Disbanded soldiers crowded into Budapest, bringing with them the accumulated fury of those four atrocious years, which had now culminated in defeat. The town throbbed with riot and revolution. His friends pressed him to leave the capital, where he was no longer safe, and to take refuge on his estates. He would not listen to them, although he entertained no illusions as to the fate which awaited him. "If the extreme party ever come to power," he said to one of his intimate friends, "their leaders will at all events agree on one point: and that is, that I should be torn in pieces and my limbs nailed up in the four corners of the town."

That day was not long in coming. Under the auspices of Count Karolyi, a National Council had been formed at Budapest, which claimed to have taken the place of the regular government. This council decided in a secret sitting that it would rid itself of the only man capable of opposing its designs. Three of its members, the Jewish journalists Kéri and Fenyès and Captain Cszerniak, an officer-deserter who had assumed the title of president of the Soldiers' Soviet, were charged to find assassins. For the sum of a hundred thousand crowns, they secured the services of a Jewish journalist, Joseph Pogany by name, of Dobo, a deserter from the army, Horvat Sanovich, a deserter from the navy, Hüttner, a lieutenant on the active list, another Jew called Gärtner, whose profession I do not know, and a few others of the same stamp. Then they waited for a favorable opportunity. During the night from October 30th to the 31st, 1918, the revolution prepared by Karolyi and his friends broke out at Budapest. Tisza rose early, as was his custom, to attend to his work. The weather was dull and damp, the little gardens of the quarter of the town where his villa was situated were chilled with fog and hoarfrost. It was a quarter which reminded one of certain corners of Neuilly or Auteuil. He learned of the events of the night from the newspapers. Soon his niece, Countess Denise Almassy, arrived. She had come on foot through a part of the town, and she did not hide from her uncle that from all she had seen on the way, there was no doubt it was desired to take his life. She implored him to leave the house without delay, to go to the country or take refuge with his friends. He thanked the countess for her solicitude, but he told her he did not wish to bring misfortune upon anyone, that he had never in his life hidden himself, and that he would die as he had lived.

Thereupon his wife gave him a letter from one of his friends who lived in the next villa, warning him that an attempt would be made upon his life and begging him to take precautions. "These things are ordained from above," he replied, with Calvinistic acceptance of the Divine Will.

He wrote two letters: one to Count Hadik, president of the council, the other to the military commandant of the town, to offer them his services. Then he looked to the condition of his revolver, arranged some papers, and burnt others. His wife implored him not to destroy anything which could justify his past or afford him a chance of escape in the present. "These documents," he replied, "are no longer of use to me, and they are very compromising for others." So he threw into the fire the copy of the letter which he had written to the emperor in July 1914, in which he urged moderation, and also the minutes of the famous Crown Council, at which he had so vainly striven to make Berchtold, Stürgkh, Bilinski, Conrad, and Krobatin, in short all those people who had in fact started the war, listen to reason.

After luncheon, which is usually served about two o'clock in Hungary, he wanted to go to his club, as was his daily habit. But in compliance with his wife's entreaties and with those of Countess Almassy, he gave up the idea. From time to time, shots were heard in the distance, fired in the town. Bands of demonstrators passed by the garden gate with insulting cries. The two women by Tisza's side awaited the outcome with agonized hearts. The dusk of evening had already fallen when, towards five o'clock, his servant entered and, in a voice stifled with emotion, told him that some armed soldiers had forced the door and asked to speak with him. Then Tisza rose from his chair, shook his servant by the hand, and said to him: "Thank you, my man, you have always been faithful to me"—as if it were a farewell. Then, revolver in hand and with a firm step, he passed into the adjoining room, followed by his wife and niece. There was a sound of voices and footsteps, and of the butts of rifles being grounded on the floor.

Three armed men were in the room, and three others stood near the door. There were also others waiting in the hall and the garden. The gendarmes, whose duty it was to protect the villa, had abandoned their charge at the first summons.

"What do you want of me?" Count Tisza asked the three men who confronted him. "We have come to judge you," said the one who seemed to have taken command of the band, "for you are the cause of the war." Another said, "It is your fault that I remained for four years in the trenches and that my wife went to the bad." And the third, addressing him as "Excellency," reproached him with his son's death.

Tisza answered them, "I deplore, like you, the immense catastrophe which has overwhelmed us, but if you were better informed, you would not accuse me in this manner."

"You lie! Besides one does not argue with a man who has a revolver in his hand. Throw down your weapon."

"Certainly," replied the count, "but you must first lay down your rifles."

"Throw down your revolver first."

Tisza hesitated for a moment, and then reflecting that if he did not obey them, a horrible massacre would follow, and that his wife and niece would fall with him, he made two steps towards the table and laid down his revolver.

"And now," said one of the murderers, pointing at Countess Tisza, "let the big woman leave the room. Your last hour has come."

Upon this the three men took aim. With one bound Count Tisza sprang forward, disengaging himself from the two women who tried to protect him with their bodies, and seized one of the rifles to prevent its being fired. But at the same moment the three rifles went off. He sank to the floor. His wife and Countess Almassy, who were slightly wounded, threw themselves upon his body. He murmured, "I knew it. It had to happen." A few moments later he died.

The story of what followed was told me by M. de Radvansky, Count Tisza's nephew. His uncle had sent him to his club to obtain news of the events that were taking place in the town. It was there he heard of the crime. He returned at once to the house, where he found the corpse still lying on the ground. He helped the servants to carry it to a bed. At that moment, an officer, who said he came from the minister of war, insisted upon being admitted. He asked first whether he could be of any use, then said that the minister had charged him to find out how the murder had happened, and finally, much embarrassed, he took an official letter from his pocket and said "I am also deputed to assure myself that His Excellency is really dead." "See for yourself," said M. de Radvansky, half opening the door and showing him the corpse lying on the bed.

The officer had hardly left when another visitor appeared. He came on behalf of the Soldiers' Committee. He also wanted to be sure that Tisza was really dead. As he had no written order he was not allowed to enter.

Two days later the mortal remains of Count Tisza were transported to the village of Geszt, where his family estate is situated and where he was to be buried. Shortly before the body was to be moved, Count Karolyi sent a funeral wreath with these words attached to it: "To my great adversary, in sign of reconciliation." Countess Tisza had these flowers thrown upon the dung heap.

The funeral cortege consisted only of three carriages, in which the members of the family had taken their places. A rumor was current that the populace wished to attack it on its way from the house to the station. Nothing, however, happened on the way, but on the platform a stone, thrown by a demonstrator, nearly hit Countess Almassy. The train which conveyed the coffin was crowded with soldiers returning to their homes. They swarmed everywhere, on the footboards, on the roofs, even on the roof of the carriage which contained Tisza's body. M. de Radvansky, who was watching by the bier, a revolver in his pocket, told me that during the whole journey he heard the soldiers over his head insulting his uncle and trampling on the roof as if they were trampling on the corpse. Another unforgettable detail: at a station where the train stopped for a few minutes they passed another train which was also filled with soldiers returning to Budapest. These men, hearing that Tisza's body was in one of the carriages, shouted, "Elyen, Elyen," which means Bravo! The two trains separated, each carrying volleys of abuse of Tisza in different directions.

At Geszt there was not a single black flag hung from the windows, as is the custom in Hungary for funerals. Only the castle bell tolled. Then even that sound ceased, for the people of the village threatened to kill the bell-ringer.

Thus Count Tisza was buried, amid the insults of men and the silence of his surroundings. His was a truly tragic personality, whose spirit, perhaps a little narrow-minded, and whose unusual firmness of soul have often recalled to my mind those great Calvinistic figures: Admiral de Coligny, the brothers de Witt, and the Scotch Puritans.

Of the five ministers who had taken part in the Imperial Council of July 7th, 1914, he was the second to die by the hand of an assassin. Count Stürgkh, prime minister of Austria, had fallen before him, shot by Adler, the socialist Jew. As for the others, their fate was less tragic. As soon as he saw that affairs were going badly, Count Berchtold fled and took refuge in Switzerland, where he continues to live the elegant life of a rich seigneur. The chevalier Krobatin is today at Graz, a charming Styrian town, situated in the midst of wooded mountains, a paradise for retired or destitute officials. Conrad de Hoetzendorf is writing his memoirs somewhere. There is always an element of comedy even in the saddest of human affairs. In this case it is supplied by Count de Bilinski, former finance minister of the Dual Monarchy, who had been so determined a supporter of war at any price, and who at its end became for a short time president of the council of an independent Poland, reconstituted by the blood of the Allies.

V

— AN AMBITIOUS MAGNATE —

Count Tisza was fond of recalling that he derived his origin from that class of small, untitled nobility, which constitutes the foundation of the Magyar aristocracy. Count Michel Karolyi prided himself, on the contrary, upon belonging to the most ancient titled nobility of Hungary. One of his ancestors fought by the side of Rakoczi II, prince of Transylvania, an ally of Louis XIV in his struggle against the Hapsburgs. When the great king made his peace with the House of Austria, and Rakoczi, abandoned to his own resources, was forced to renounce the struggle and retire to Versailles, it was this same Karolyi who negotiated the ill-omened peace of Szathmar with the emperor, thus consecrating the defeat of Hungary's supreme effort to throw off the sovereignty of Austria. In gratitude for that service, the emperor gave him the hereditary title of count. Since that time the family has never ceased to play a great part in the affairs of the Dual Monarchy and to acquire immense possessions.

At the age of twenty, Michel Karolyi possessed a princely fortune. He had inherited a hundred thousand hectares of entailed estates, another property of four thousand acres which was situated one hour from Budapest, and a magnificent mansion in the very heart of the town, which was surrounded by lovely gardens, an inexpressible boon to that city, so devoid of gardens and verdure. He was a singular youth. The origin of his peculiarities may perhaps be sought in a physiological defect. "Distrust deformed men," says the Bible.

Karolyi was a deformed man. His mouth was deformed from his birth and until he was eight or ten years old he could hardly articulate. He was given an artificial palate, but his conversation always remained a somewhat confused stammering, which was rapidly converted into a kind of bark if he raised his voice. From his earliest days he must have suffered much from such an obvious infirmity. This is clearly shown in his remarkable confidences as to his own childish sentiments. Yet they were the confidences of a rich child surrounded by every luxury. "From my earliest years," he said one day, "my greatest desire was to make a revolution." Surely this was the nightmare of a sick child, quick to conceive a horror of the world and to feel nothing but hatred and dislike for all that was normal or healthily constituted.

As a young man he tried to hide his misfortune by a passion for all violent forms of sport, so that he might give an impression of being an exceptionally vigorous person.

But in this very violence the fatal blemish of his character appeared. One of his youthful companions, Count Teleki, said to me: "It is the absence of all moderation that characterizes Michel"—his excess in everything, and the ridiculous failure which invariably followed all he undertook. If he went out shooting, he would arrive in English clothes in the most eccentric taste, thus surprising the guests and causing the keepers and beaters to laugh in their sleeves. Of course, his gun was of the latest fashion, but it was in vain that he fired off numberless cartridges; he always missed the game. If he took part in a game of polo, he was indeed a redoubtable opponent, for while he invariably missed the ball, he frequently broke the ponies' legs. He was the wildest card player in the kingdom (and heaven knows what that means in Hungary), but there again fortune usually turned against him.

He would lose hundreds of thousands of crowns in one game, and despite his riches he was always deeply in debt. Being desperately fond of speed, he held the record for automobile accidents. Finally his morbid desire for new sensations led him to commit great excesses. "Cannot you understand," he said to Countess Teleki, "that for my taste, what makes the whole zest of life is to find myself continually confronted with some new and unexpected sensation." This frame of mind may be possible for a fine gentleman solely occupied with his own pleasure, but it is likely to carry a great seigneur, who cherishes the ambition of directing his country's affairs, further than he intended.

It was impossible that the count should not have nourished that ambition. In his eyes politics must necessarily have appeared as the first of all sports for a man of his rank. Since time immemorial the highest aristocracy has always directed public affairs at Budapest. If the strange house of Orczi has a claim to be considered as the symbol of the triumphant Judaism of Pest, the National Casino—the club frequented by the nobility—assuredly represents the power of the Magyar aristocracy. It stands in the Kossuth Lajos Utca, the most brilliant street of the town, a perfectly simple house which is a relief to the eye among huge buildings that are a perfect nightmare of brick and cement. There, for nearly a century, amidst the hum of conversation and the buzz of card parties, far more than in the Parliament or the Chamber of Magnates, Hungarian politics have been made. The highborn Magyars who met there daily were almost in complete accord in their ideas and prejudices. Nearly all of them could boast that their father or their grandfather had fought against Austria in 1848 in the War of Independence; but they had ended by following Count Tisza's example and accepting the necessity to live in a good understanding with Vienna and also Berlin, which incidentally gave them many advantages.

The Triple Alliance seemed to them the only safe way of combating the Russian menace; and in the midst of a Europe which, to their ideas, was becoming too rapidly democratized, they saw a providential ally in Germany, who would help them to maintain as long as possible the feudal character of Hungary. In this their country strikingly resembles France before 1789, with its immense seigneurial domains extending often to fifty or a hundred thousand hectares, about equally divided between the laity and the ecclesiastical mortmain properties, or such as pay the state ridiculously small dues, and with its provincial assemblies, where the influence of the clergy and the nobles predominated.

It was a matter of course that Michel Karolyi should belong to the National Casino. He played there and he lost, and the debts which be accumulated robbed him of much of the prestige which his immense fortune had given him. No one took this inveterate gambler seriously, this rake who had such a great longing to shine in political discussions. The defect in his palate and his barking voice were greatly in the way of his success. He sought, as usual, to surmount his infirmity by making himself peculiar, and to attain importance by ostentatiously brushing aside the opinions generally accepted around him. He declared himself in favor of universal suffrage and demanded an agrarian reform which would have divided the seigneurial domains among the peasants. As regards foreign policy, he had adopted the views of the old party of 1848. This party, which numbered only about ten of the deputies, was resolutely hostile to Austria and to Germany—in theory at least—for in practice it often weakened in this opinion. It wished to break with the Triple Alliance, it manifested sympathy with France when occasion offered, and was averse to all idea of war, of which the result, it considered, could only harm the Magyars, for if they were victorious they would be more than ever subservient to the Germans, and if they were beaten they would be sure to see their country's territory diminished and the Slav supremacy established in Central Europe.

In his adherence to these ideas, Karolyi was in tune with the old instincts of his race and with his family traditions. His grandfather, Batthyany, who was president of the council in 1848, had been shot by the Austrians, and his grandmother ignobly flogged on the public square, by Marshal Haynau's soldiers. Allied as he himself was to the Dillons and the Polignacs, it was natural that his sympathies should be with France. Ideas are valued according to the men who represent them. Perhaps it was not altogether fortunate for France that Count Michel Karolyi should be her champion in Hungary.

One can easily imagine that profound antipathy should characterize two such opposite natures as Karolyi and Tisza. The one perfectly balanced, with a peasant robustness, passionate, certain of power, devoid of mean vanity and defending, not without a certain grandeur, that sinister German policy which was destined to be as fatal to his country as to himself. The other, unwholesome, full of unrest and of a mad desire to cut a figure in the world, less interested in ideas for their intrinsic merit and justice than for the support they might give him in his quest of power. Tisza despised Karolyi as an unhappy, restless soul; Karolyi envied Tisza for his natural eloquence and, above all, his prestige: that mysterious gift of authority which comes no one knows whence, and which no man possesses unless the gods themselves have endowed him with it at his birth.

Some years before the war, a violent altercation in the Chamber led these two men to engage in a duel. Tisza, who was the elder by twenty years, parried the sword thrusts and riposted with coolness and precision. Thirty-five times he amused himself by touching his adversary with the flat of his sword. That evening after the duel, he merely said at his club, "Karolyi fought very well." It was only during the last months of his life, when he realized the detestable influence which the unbalanced young man would have upon his country, that he said to his nephew (who repeated it to the writer), "I begin to think that I did wrong in not killing Michel on that day long ago."

In the spring of 1914 the chief of the party of 1848, Francis Kossuth, died. He was a man of rather mediocre ability, crushed by the great name which he bore and full of secret complaisance for the government of which he declared himself an enemy. Karolyi seized the opportunity to become the head of the party. He elaborated immediately a vast scheme of propaganda with the object of overthrowing the system of alliances and of detaching Hungary from Germany. Several deputies were detailed to go to Petrograd and Paris and get into touch there with the Russian and French politicians. He himself, accompanied by Stephen Friedrich, his secretary, and a few friends, sailed for America, hoping to gain over to his view the two millions of Magyar emigrants in the United States and collect enough money for the prosecution of his enterprise.

Having finished his tour, which had not been without some success, he was returning to Europe when he heard on board ship of the declaration of war. At Bordeaux he and his suite were interned as belonging to an enemy country. He, however, quickly obtained his release from the French government and returned to Budapest by way of Spain and Genoa, after having given an undertaking not to fight against France.

So long as the German successes maintained in the imagination of the people the certainty of victory, his role was played completely in the background. He contented himself with deploring the peace which he then foresaw, a conqueror's peace, which, he said, would force Hungary to surround herself with trenches as large as the Danube, and which her whole population would not suffice to defend. After Verdun, however, and the Somme, when the German triumph seemed less secure, and especially when Russia had retired from the struggle, his popularity with the rural population increased rapidly. Once the Muscovite armies were out of the running, the war ceased to have any meaning for the Hungarian peasants. In their eyes, they were only being called upon to fight for the detested Germans, whom they hated all the more fiercely now for obliging them to let themselves be killed for no reason. Villagers and soldiers were alike grateful to Karolyi because he had always been hostile to the people in power at Vienna and Berlin, and in Hungary, subjugated as it was to the German will and that of the "generals," as they were called, he began to appear as the one man capable of realizing the immense desire for peace which lay deep down in the hearts of all the people.

At Budapest there rallied round him a few intellectuals, radicals, freemasons, and socialists, for the most part Jews, who all collaborated more or less in the production of two advanced reviews, whose influence had been considerable in Hungary during the last fifteen years. The first one, entirely sociological in its scope, the *Huszadik Szazad* (*The Twentieth Century*), had taken as its mission the task of spreading the most modern ideas concerning social organization. The other, which was entirely literary, the *Nyugat* (*The West*) endeavored to make known the latest intellectual ideas of Western Europe. Oscar Jaszi, who for twenty years had defended, not without intelligence and generosity, the national minorities so often maltreated in Hungary, edited *The Twentieth Century*. I knew him well in old days when he was following the university course.

He was an excellent young man, but quite wrapped up in his books; a harmless lunatic, a dreamer, and a hundred miles distant from real life. The following anecdote seems to me to hit him off exactly. He had lately become a father. Noticing one day that his son was being brought up by a wet nurse, and considering the question of cause and effect, he said to himself that this beautiful beribboned peasant woman must also have a child of her own. He asked her what she had done with it. The woman replied that she had left it in her village. How could a humanitarian socialist take part in such an iniquity? Jaszi at once sent for the child and commanded the woman to feed both infants. Three months afterwards they were both dead. He committed the same kind of error some time later, when, having become minister of nationalities, he ordered the equal distribution of arms to the Magyars and Romanian peasants of Transylvania, in order that they might defend their mountains. The result of such a policy made itself quickly felt. An appalling orgy of slaughter broke out in the whole province between the villagers of different race.

Louis Hatvany, who sprang from a rich, Jewish family of bankers and sugar merchants, was the inspirer and financier of *Nyugat*. When I knew him twenty years ago, he only read French books and considered no one superior to Sainte-Beuve. Of a lively disposition and an enthusiast, he was always ready to discover a misunderstood genius and to assist him. How many pleasant hours have I spent in the old seigneurial house, which his father had bought at Hatvan and the name of which he had taken, or else at Buda in the Directoire confectioner's shop with its gilded compote dishes and its Winged Victories! A few years later I saw him again during the short stay he made in Paris. His tastes had changed. He still preserved his juvenile enthusiasm in which once recognized that feverishness and neurasthenic activity so often to be met with persons of his race, but he had taken a dislike to our literature, which was too reasonable for his taste, and only found pleasure in the most modern German literary works. He hardly ever left Berlin and I remember that he cited to me as incontestable geniuses a mass of unknown Teutons who filled the young reviews there with their prose and their verse, and who, according to him, put all our French writers, with the exception of Charles-Louis Philippe, into the shade.

Under the color of modernism, Louis Hatvany and his

friends of the *Nyugat* had deliberately broken from all the intellectual and moral traditions which made pastoral and agricultural Hungary an ancient and noble country, to which men's hearts attach themselves as do ours to our Provence. All the typical characters which, until yesterday, animated the works of the Magyar writers, have disappeared and been obliterated from their ephemeral literature. One searches in vain for Jokai's romantic figures, for the heavy, proud, and self-willed seigneurs of Baron Kemenyi, or for the melancholy or gay peasants of the exquisite Coloman Mikszath. Their productions, befogged by an antiquated symbolism, which reminds one of an old clothes shop, contain nothing that recalls the inimitable accents, now despairing, now joyous of the Hungarian songs, where dreams and tears mingle on the borders of ecstasy. Nowhere does one feel the balmy breath of air which from all parts of the plain makes the acacia leaves tremble and carries away the dust raised by the flocks of sheep. No echo responds to Petofi's songs of love or of war; no flute chimes in with the bucolic music of Arany. I know that it would be deplorable if our dreams of today were like children's clothes cut out from the dresses of their ancestors, but a literature must continue something, and this new literature continues nothing at all. Apart from the great poet Ady, the despairing singer of twilight Hungary and who belonged to the old Magyar gentry, these poets, these romancers, these essayists, who fill the pages of *Nyugat*, do not portray the true, rustic Hungary, but paint it in the colors of Budapest. They are like those big town houses on the banks of the Danube which hurt the eye and overwhelm the spirit by their ridiculous proportions and pretentious facades, and which reflect the Jewish spirit in all its feverish idealism and its instinctive revolt against the modes of thought and feeling, which have been detested by them and their ancestors for two thousand years. Their intellectual efforts, combined with the activity of the men on the stock exchange or who are engaged in trade, have ended in making Budapest a sort of vast mart of Semitic ideas and interests, where the real national thought is disfigured, and where the dreams of the West take on as by a horrible miracle the gabardine of the house of Orczi and speak in Yiddish!

In this setting the Russian revolution appeared as the dawn of that great evening which Israel has awaited for centuries. Tentative as it still was, Kerensky's revolution opened up prodigious horizons for those Jewish imaginations, who only understand working at a gallop. With the knowledge they possessed, placed in direct contact with their Russian brothers by that long river of Judaism, which passing from Petrograd, by Bielostock, Vilna, and Lemberg, comes down to Budapest, they knew well that it was only a beginning, that the movement would not end there and that in the northern plains unheard-of upheavals were preparing, of which the effect, overflowing the Russian frontiers, would extend to the whole of Europe and upset the entire existing social order from top to bottom. At least, that was what they hoped.

Such were the ideas which in the spring of 1917 filled the salons of the Palais Karolyi and the somewhat empty head of their owner. In all these Orientals bewitched by the West, this great seigneur admired a culture which seemed to him all the more magnificent because he was very ignorant, and an audaciousness of thought which flattered his unbalanced temperament. On their side, these intellectual Jews (who were not all possessed of fortunes like Jaszi or Hatvany) allowed themselves to be dazzled by this ultrarich magnate who was ready to receive them and treat them as equals. The praises which they lavished on him served to reinforce the already exaggerated opinion which he entertained of his political genius. The more astute ones made money out of him. Little by little he became the center of all the hopes of those who awaited a social cataclysm in the near future, or peace at any price, or quite simply alms.

His wife, Countess Michel, who was likewise ambitious and modern to the tips of her fingers, had also a court in which a crowd of overexcited Jewesses, feminists, or pacifists, were to be met. From whence had Catherine Karolyi picked up this taste for ideas and persons so foreign to her class? Certainly not from her father! He was Count Julius Andrassy, and the very type of a great Hungarian nobleman such as was to be met with at the Nemetzi Casino, entirely devoted to the Hapsburgs, very faithful to the German alliance, and profoundly attached to his privileges as a noble. She herself, an aristocrat such as one finds in Eastern Europe, in Hungary, in Poland, and in Russia, affords an example of those women who, while they reap the benefit of the immense advantages which their fortune and name procure for them, find a sort of voluptuous pleasure in placing themselves outside their own caste and playing with opinions destructive of all they love. There is certainly foolishness, but above all great conceit, in this naive infatuation for ideas of which they are first of all the dupes, and of which they often end by being the victims. We also in France remember the beautiful, giddy women who, before 1789, were enthusiastic about principles which led them to the scaffold.

As Michel Karolyi made much of the relations he had established during the course of his famous voyage with the principal politicians of the Entente, Count Czernin, minister for foreign affairs in the Dual Monarchy, lit upon the idea of sending him to Switzerland when it began to dawn upon him that it would be necessary for Austria to make a separate peace. The result was piteous in the extreme. Karolyi sent before him a harbinger to prepare the way for his mission, an extravagant personage whom he subsequently made his minister for foreign affairs, his friend Diener Denes. This Jew kept a reading room in Budapest and had devoured all the books in it himself; his brain in consequence had become a curious replica of one of those libraries organized for the general reader. He himself was the author of a work on Leonardo da Vinci, whom he said he had long failed to understand, until one day he made the discovery of his genius by the light of Karl Marx! He wore a yellow wig on his head; the wig was always crooked, and his ideas were the same.

From the first moment of his arrival in Switzerland, Diener Denes took pains to get into touch with Guilbeaux and the most notorious defeatists, no matter to what nation they belonged, many of whom were then carrying on an agitation in Geneva. He had already awakened the suspicions of the representatives of the Entente when Karolyi joined him. Denes' Bolshevist views could only strengthen the credulous magnate in his belief that the world revolution was at hand. In his spare time the count amused himself and frequented the gaming houses that had multiplied at a rapid rate in Calvin's ancient city. When he asked for an audience with the British minister he was received by a simple vice-consul. As to our minister M. Beau, it appears that he asked: "Is he a buffoon or an influential man?"

"He is," they told him, "an influential buffoon."

So he refused to see him.

The longer the war went on, the more did the Germans make the weight of their domination felt at Budapest. At the same time Count Karolyi's popularity continued to increase and Stephen Tisza's as rapidly diminished. In Berlin they considered Karolyi a dangerous person whom it was time to compromise. A colonel who had accomplished wonders by spying in Turkey was charged with the mission. He approached one of the count's secretaries, whom he knew to be an impecunious gambler, so as to get from him his patrons' correspondence in return for a large sum of money. The secretary was an honest man. He warned Karolyi and arranged with him that he should appear to accept the German's proposal and fix a rendezvous. The two men met, ostensibly in order to arrange the terms of the contract, but at the end of the interview two witnesses, who had been concealed, opened the door of a room next to the one in which the interview had taken place and told the colonel that they had taken down a report of the whole conversation. This affair was noised abroad and further increased Michel Karolyi's prestige among the Hungarian people, who were exasperated by the domineering manners which the Germans increasingly assumed towards them. They now began to see that Hungary was being sacrificed to Germany.

The breakup on the Bulgarian front, Ludendorff's retreat in France, and the inevitable crumbling of the Austro-Hungarian forces all seemed to justify this view. In Parliament Karolyi proclaimed that the safety of the country demanded that Germany should be abandoned to her fate; that they must lay down their arms before they were invaded and confide their interests to President Wilson; that they must carry out at the earliest possible moment great democratic reforms so as to engage Western sympathy on Hungary's behalf. Such words in a Parliament which was still dominated by the loyalist spirit of Tisza appeared sacrilegious. Some deputies threatened to box his ears; they even talked of putting him on his trial. But outside the Parliament his speeches awakened profound echoes, which were prolonged in hearts suffering from apprehension of the terrible unknown. He made the impression of a prophet who, if only they would have listened to him, would have warded off from his country the misfortunes which were falling upon her, and in the general crumbling away of everything they saw in him the only man capable of saving that which still might be saved. From day to day and from hour to hour, as the collapse became more imminent, all the hatred which was gathering round Count Tisza added to Karolyi's popularity. And finally he was carried to power by the exasperation of the people in pursuit of their old, undying desire for an independent Hungary, which should be forever free from Austrian domination.

On October 22nd, the fact of the Bulgarian capitulation became known. The following day, in the middle of a parliamentary sitting, came the news that some mutinous Croatian troops had taken possession of Fiume, the great Hungarian port on the Adriatic. Karolyi mounted the tribune and declared that the catastrophe was now complete, while some Jewish journalists (who a few weeks later revealed themselves as ardent internationalists) led a fearful uproar, demanding the resignation of the Minister Weckerle in the name of the violated country.

On the same day at Debrecen, where the king and queen had gone to inaugurate the new university, the populace hissed the regiments of the Austrian Guard that were on duty as the Guard of Honor and howled down the imperial national anthem which the hand had had the unlucky idea of playing instead of the royal (Hungarian) national anthem. At Kaschau the regiment of which William II was colonel threw down their arms. At Budapest the thirty-second Regiment of Infantry, which had been created by Maria Theresa, slept in their barrack yard, this being the usual method by which Hungarian soldiers declare mutiny. And by every train there arrived thousands of emaciated, ragged deserters from the Italian front, who threw away their rifles crying "We are tired of dying for these Germans who make slaves of us."

At the Hotel Astoria, one of the largest hotels in the town (the hotels and the cafes always took the first place during this Hungarian Revolution, as they do in the ordinary life of Budapest), Karolyi and his friends had already formed the National Council, like those which had been constituted at Prague, Lemberg, and Agram, and in all the provinces which, in reliance upon President Wilson's principles, aspired to become independent states. This council, which consisted of about thirty members, had taken as their president a priest, the Abbe Hock, a sort of Jerome Coignard, with whom in old days I had drunk many pots of beer and glasses of sham Tokay as we listened to the gypsy band.

This lover of taverns was of imposing stature, with a long face and strongly marked features, magnificent eyes of the color of Spanish tobacco and a sensual mouth, which was unfortunately spoiled by villainous teeth, but he was the personification of eloquence. Thirty years ago, the court and all the elegant world of Budapest—not excepting the rich Jewesses—flocked to hear his sermons in the Cathedral of Buda. But his successes with the fair sex became too notorious and unfortunately interrupted his triumphs as a preacher. He was exiled to a parish in the suburbs and got himself elected a deputy. Since then he had divided his time between his flock in the slums, the lobbies of the Chamber, the editing of a newspaper, and the cafes of the town.

The first act of this council was to launch a manifesto requiring the mediate return of the National Army, the signing of an armistice, the liberty of nationalities within the state, and the maintenance of the integrity of the country within the limits which had bounded it for more than a thousand years. The manifesto was signed by Karolyi, and the revolutionary count begged the foreign governments to address themselves in future to him alone and not to the moribund royal government.

Meanwhile the king had returned to Budapest, or rather to Godollo, a little castle surrounded by a large garden, situated three quarters of an hour distant from the town. He was anxious and upset and consulted everybody; then, after much hesitation, and despite the advice of his counsellors, he finally decided to send for Karolyi. Karolyi hastened to Godollo, convinced that his hour had come.

When he arrived there, the castle was filled by an unusual crowd. There were there, strangely intermingled, magnates, peasant delegates from the great plain, industrials, and merchants whom the sovereign had summoned in order that he might form an idea of the opinion of the country—among others the bishop of Transylvania, the parish priest of St. Mathias of Buda, the confessor of the imperial family, generals, colonels, one admiral, court ladies, maids of honor, and Red Cross nurses. Most of these people saw the arrival of the man who, in their eyes, represented the spirit of the revolution, with no friendly feeling. But when Count Hunyadi, grand master of ceremonies, approached Karolyi in order to introduce him to the august presence, they all made a deferential lane for the passage of this democratic seigneur, who no doubt would become the all-powerful master of tomorrow.

The king, who had never had any special sympathy with Tisza or the former members of the Hungarian Parliament, did not reject the idea of confiding the formation of a ministry to Karolyi. He conversed with him for nearly an hour and a half. But while he was speaking, Prince Windischgraetz telephoned to him from Vienna urging him to be cautious. Charles hung up the receiver and continued his conversation. He detained his guest to dine with him, and Karolyi must certainly have thought that evening that on the morrow he would be president of the council.

The same evening, about ten o'clock, he found himself suddenly face to face with the queen in one of the drawing rooms. Without any preamble she said to him, in excited tones:

"Count, you must help us. You must help the emperor, my husband, your king. They tell me that you are going to make a revolution, that Hungary is going to disown us. Count, you would not do that? It would be too horrible, save him! He is such an excellent man."

And with these words the empress-queen left the room before her surprised hearer had time to open his mouth.

A few moments later the king said to Karolyi: "Count, I must positively return to Vienna, where the situation has become very disquieting. Come with us. The train is waiting. We will arrange the affairs of Hungary there, for you will help me, will you not?"

Karolyi bowed and took his place in the royal railway

carriage. During the journey he had ample opportunity of observing that there was hardly anyone of the party, excepting the emperor, who was not hostile to him.

On arriving in Vienna, Charles took leave of him with much cordiality and begged him to hold himself in readiness for a summons. But it was in vain that Karolyi awaited his sovereign's message all the next day at the Hotel Bristol. Towards four o'clock he sent to ask the grand master of the court what was the meaning of this silence. The grand master replied that he had better return to Budapest, and that the archduke Joseph, who had been nominated *homo regius*, that is to say, representative of the king in Hungary, would communicate to him His Majesty's decisions. Evidently Prince Windischgraetz's counsels had finally prevailed. The will to resist had conquered the king's half-hearted liberal tendencies.

The following morning Karolyi returned to Budapest. An eyewitness, a French officer who was a prisoner in Hungary, drew for me a picture of this return:

"I have never seen such a sight as I witnessed that day. An immense, silent crowd waited around the Western railway station. The multitude was almost motionless but was traversed now and again by slow currents and deep eddies. Above the silence and the heavy swell of the human bodies, immense banners were displayed, scarlet, brick-colored, bloodred, wine red or purple, a whole gamut of violent tones which contrasted strangely with the somber mass of the people and the grey damp skies. Suddenly this mass opened to let the 'Friends of the People' pass. These were Marton de Lovaszy, who one day in the Chamber of Deputies had dared to cry 'We are the friends of the Entente; long live republican France; long live liberty,' and had nearly been hanged for it; then the Socialist Garami, editor of the journal *Nepszava*, 'The Voice of the People'; the social democrat Bokanyi, and Colonel Lindner. Others followed, their names being shouted by the people as they passed. At last the train arrived. The crowd pushed, crushed together in a kind of fury, but always in extraordinary silence. Suddenly a prodigious clamor, a perfect roar arose. Handkerchiefs, branches of oak and pine, and flags of the national colors were waved; Karolyi had appeared on the station platform. In him they saluted madly the liberator of Hungary. He spoke with jerky gesticulations. No one heard what he said, but they applauded him all the same. Marton de Lovaszy shouted to him: 'Take the power. You will hold it from the people if not from the king.'

"'Citizens,' screamed a powerful voice, 'we have one more enemy now, it is King Charles.' Not long ago such a speech would have caused a police charge and blood would have flowed; today it only aroused applause. Karolyi got into his carriage. All of a sudden I felt a lump in my throat and my eyes grew misty. The crowd was singing, and despite the strange words and the slower cadence I recognized the 'Marseillaise'! The song that crowd was singing was the song of my country, which I had not heard for four years. It is the sublime cry of my race, which for these people meant liberty and for me victory! It was a magnificent moment, which for a second raised me, a useless prisoner of war, to the height of all my brothers in the trenches. I was so filled with emotion that I seemed to be lifted beyond the present day, above that multitude and above myself. Then shaken, pushed, and roughly handled, I allowed myself to be carried along on that human tide, and my voice mingled with the voices of all those Magyars—'The day of glory has arrived!'"

The king chose Count Hadik to form a ministry instead of Karolyi. He was a colorless creature without any prestige. He tried to negotiate with the different parties of the National Council so as to sow dissension among them and thus cause its dissolution. But the assembly declared unanimously that no party would enter into a separate negotiation. While Hadik was painfully endeavoring to form a cabinet with some obscure deputies and functionaries who were known for their reactionary spirit, Budapest and the whole country rallied with transports of joy round the National Assembly, which at that moment represented Hungarian independence and the desire for immediate peace. All the great public services, the industries, the banks, the universities, and the police gave in their allegiance. The money which had been collected a short time previously in the United States, and which most opportunely arrived in Budapest by way of Switzerland, was lavishly distributed to the workmen and soldiers in order to inflame their enthusiasm. The National Council was encouraged, though perhaps somewhat embarrassed by so sudden a success; it now deliberated as to the day on which it should establish the new regime in Hungary. Someone proposed November 1st, but it was All Saints' Day and it seemed impossible to make a revolution on that day. The following day, Saturday, was payday and was equally unsuitable. Then came Sunday, a general holiday, which was also unacceptable. They decided on Monday, November 4th. But the event did not wait for the National Council's order.

VI

— THE END OF THE HAPSBURGS —

"Where and when the revolution began I do not know." That is a statement which Michel Karolyi is ever ready to repeat when he is asked about a movement with which his name will always remain associated, as will that of Kerensky with the overthrow of tzarism.

On October 29th, about ten o'clock in the evening, several thousand men met in Andrassy Street in order to ascend the hill of Buda to the palace of the archduke Joseph, make a demonstration there against the *homo regius*, and demand that Karolyi should be their minister president. But the military governor had barred the bridges, and the royal gendarmes and the mounted police fired upon the assailants, who were in consequence obliged to retire, leaving four dead and about forty wounded in the fray.

The next day there began to appear on the walls enormous posters, imitated from Russia, which, under the Bolshevik regime, were to cover the whole town with bloodred color and with outrageous symbolism. Some of them represented a formidable red workman brandishing a monstrous chopper above the fragments of the royal crown; others portrayed a soldier strangling the Hapsburg double eagle with his hands; others displayed, in letters of flame, a vehement ballad inviting the army to make a compact with the people, of which the refrain was, "Do not fire, O my son! I am there in the crowd."

At night, about one o'clock in the morning, someone, no one knows who, but probably the journalist Gondor, whose real name was Nathan Krauss (he was formerly apprenticed to a furrier in America and was a man of violent temperament, whose mouth was always full of curses), threw out, no one knows where, the idea of taking possession of the military quarters. Although it was raining in torrents, a certain number of people who happened to be in the streets started off to march there by the light of torches that flickered in the rain. Before the building the police guard threw up their arms. Accompanied by a few unknown men, a Jewish dancer, who was also a swindler (his name was Heltai), presented himself in tennis shoes to the commandant of the palace. The latter was an old Austrian general, almost alone in the barracks; he made no resistance and yielded his post to the dancer.

Meanwhile another Jew, called Jetvai, with ten men, seized the central telephone station. When General Lukasics, the commandant of the garrison, received this news, he telephoned to the imperial headquarters at Baden, near Vienna, and asked to speak to the emperor. It was eleven minutes past three in the morning. An aide-de-camp replied that His Majesty was sleeping.

"Let him be awakened," said the general.

The king rose and came to the telephone, and Lukasics explained to him that he could get the better of the outbreak, but as it could not be done without some bloodshed he asked for orders.

"No, no," cried the king. "I will not have the people fired upon!"

No doubt, when he spoke in this way, Charles was obeying the same instinct which had made him say a few days earlier, when it was a question of deciding whether a really energetic general should be placed at the head of the garrison in Vienna:

"Certainly not; I will not have your general! It is time that force and compulsion should disappear. Enough blood has been shed. I do not propose to begin a new war against my own people. Let them organize themselves as they will."

Perhaps also he was anxious for the safety of his children, who had remained behind in the castle of Godollo, for three minutes after this interview the grand master of the court telephoned that they were to return to Vienna.

When, in the small hours of the morning, Karolyi reached his house, he found a troop of sailors in front of his door, who at once began to cheer him. Noticing, with some surprise, that there were no Magyars among them, and that they were all Dalmatians, Croatians, and Istrians, he asked them if they had come to Budapest to fight for Hungarian independence. They replied that they had no idea of the kind, they had come on account of the revolution: "Because, for a sailor, the revolution," they said, "is the essential thing!"

During the course of that morning, Charles at length decided to confide to Karolyi the task of forming a ministry. Karolyi summoned some of the members of the '48 party, some radicals and two socialists. Then he took the oath of fidelity by telephone, and once more assured the king of his devotion to the Crown.

In the street more and more soldiers from the front gathered together and acclaimed the republic. Mounted on motor lorries, which were decorated with chrysanthemums (autumn roses, as they are called in Budapest), with flowers stuck in their caps, and a red cockade on their breasts, they fired their rifles in the air and sang popular songs. It was at once an idyllic and a warlike scene, at once a drama and a comic opera, savoring of a riot and likewise of a carnival. They danced and drank—less, however, than might have been expected, as the National Council had forbidden the sale of wine and alcohol. Many red banners and flags waved above the crowd; bunches of chrysanthemums were attached to the top of the flagpoles instead of the Austrian eagle. These funereal flowers were everywhere displayed and later gave the somewhat ill-omened name of "the Revolution of the Autumn Rose" to those days, in which all the past was engulfed. Some groups went to the railway stations and took possession of the trains in order to return to their homes; others seized the boats moored along the Danube, so as to regain their villages by water; all carried off their arms with them, saying, "they will be useful against the Jews and the lawyers." Young girls tore off the badges from the officers' uniforms, either pulling them off or quietly cutting them out with scissors. The officers let them have their way; one of them who resisted was killed. Bands of pillagers threw themselves on the military stores. The crowd invaded the Western railway station, burnt the German noticeboards, and opposed the departure of a company of soldiers who were being sent to reinforce the front. That evening, in the dusk, Tisza was assassinated in the presence of his wife and niece.

At that moment the emperor was at Schönbrunn. At eleven o'clock in the evening Prince Louis Windischgraetz went from Vienna to the castle. Although it was not yet very late, no lights were visible in the windows. The immense place, plunged in darkness, appeared to be uninhabited. The prince records in his memoirs (which, though they only date back to yesterday, already seem centuries old) that he mounted to the antechamber of the Imperial Cabinet without encountering a living soul. Not a soldier was on guard, not a single lackey on duty. The great state apartments were deserted. The luxurious pomp by which the emperor was usually surrounded had disappeared. The generals, the field marshals, the higher clergy, and the aristocracy had followed the servants' example and abandoned their master. Conrad von Hoetzendorff, who had recently accepted the highly paid office of Commander of the Life Guards, had fled in the hour of danger. No doubt tonight he was sleeping peacefully in his castle at Villach in Carinthia. The prince said to himself, as he traversed that extraordinary desert: "Where are today the Lobkowitzes, the Auerspergs, the Clams, and the Schwarzenbergs, the Czemins, and the Esterhazys? Where are the Zichys, the Batthyanys, the Fesztetics, the Kinskys, all those noble seigneurs of Austria and Hungary, who for centuries have knelt on the steps of the throne and lived on the royal favor?"

Then there came back to him also the remembrance of the last festivity given in honor of the king's birthday. It had taken place on August 17th at Reichenau, hardly three months before, in the villa Wartholz. The Knights of the Order of Maria Theresa were seated around the Table of Honor. Conrad von Hoetzendorff glorified His Majesty's virtues in pompous terms. Then all of a sudden the Knights had risen to their feet, making their spurs ring and drawing their swords from the scabbards. And while they swore to be faithful to their king till death, the band played, "Gott erhalte. . . ." Tonight all was solitude and silence. The emperor-king was alone, completely alone, in his palace at Schönbrunn. Prince Windischgraetz at last reached the antechamber which gave access to the emperor. In the vast, empty apartment, there was only one aide-de-camp, reading.

"His Majesty awaits you," he said to the prince, and he ushered Windischgraetz into the apartment known as the Gobelin Salon. After they had exchanged a few words on the diplomatic situation: "Well," said the emperor, "you hear that they have just assassinated Tisza! It is a terrible thing!"

He pronounced these words quite coolly, never having cared very much for the Hungarian premier.

"Allow me," said Windischgraetz, "to warn you once more against Michel Karolyi."

"No," interrupted Charles, "Karolyi is an honest man. The Hungarian people are with him. We must second his efforts with all our power. He is now prime minister and I have ordered that the troops should be placed at his disposal."

Then the prince asked if Karolyi had taken the oath of allegiance.

"Yes," answered the king laughing, "and I think it must certainly be the first time that a minister has taken the oath by telephone."

But on the following day, Karolyi purposely exaggerated the state of unrest which reigned at Budapest and represented to the king that a new revolution had broken out. He asked to be absolved from his oath. The archduke Joseph told me that he was in the room when Karolyi was telephoning. At the end of a few moments, Karolyi hung up the receiver, saying that His Majesty had released him from his oath. This meant the recognition of Hungary's independence. The compact which united the Kingdom of St. Stephen to the Hapsburg Empire was henceforward abolished. That which the struggles of many centuries had been unable to realize had now been accomplished in a simple and commonplace manner—by telephone.

Two hours later, Windischgraetz and Julius Andrassy, minister for foreign affairs and father-in-law of Karolyi, presented themselves about midday to the emperor at Schönbrunn. The door of his cabinet was open, and they saw he was at the telephone and appeared greatly agitated. The empress stood like a statue beside him. Becoming aware of his visitors, Charles made them a sign to enter.

"I am talking with Budapest," he said nervously. "Imagine, they are now asking me to abdicate in my own name and in that of my successors!"

On hearing this, Windischgraetz snatched the receiver from the emperor's hand to prevent his continuing the conversation. Charles made no movement to resist him.

"What shall I answer? What line shall I take?" he asked. "Only this morning I absolved Karolyi from his oath. That was my last concession. Now they want me to abdicate.

They are cowards to abandon me. But I shall not abdicate. I have no right to. What these gentlemen choose to do with the oath they swore to me is their concern. As for me I shall not break the oath which I took."

Julius Andrassy was dumbfounded to find that his son-in-law was betraying his sovereign, and murmured, "is it possible he should have sunk so low!" and Windischgraetz tried to demonstrate that this Hungarian revolution was entirely artificial and should not be yielded to.

"I am not of your opinion," replied the emperor, and, indulgent, as he always was, he added: "The revolution has turned Karolyi's brain."

Andrassy then took up the telephone, which stood on the same table at which Napoleon once sat in days gone by, and upon which during the past four years of war so many important papers had been signed.

"Are you mad, that you should demand the king's abdication," he shouted down the telephone, speaking to Count Batthyany, minister of the interior in Karolyi's cabinet, and until quite recently minister of the imperial household. Batthyany replied:

"If he does not abdicate, we shall dismiss him like a bad servant."

Revolution in Hungary, revolution in Vienna, the emperor-king was no longer safe anywhere. Windischgraetz proposed to him to retire to the Tyrol with his wife and children, but the empress Zita, who kept quite cool, objected, saying:

"We must show the people that we remain where it is our duty to remain. Our place is not even here at Schönbrunn, it is in Vienna. It is there that we must go and calmly await events, without taking any further part in the matter." At this moment the chief of the general staff appeared, General Arz. In the tone of polite indifference which was habitual to him, he announced that the negotiations for an armistice with the high Italian command had been begun.

"Do any troops still remain faithful to us?" asked the king.

Arz made a negative sign with his head, and with the air of a fatalist he added:

"Sire, nothing remains to be done—all is now lost."

The Viennese proclaimed the republic a few days afterwards. The Magyars, on their part, demanded King Charles' abdication. On November 12th, five delegates arrived at Eckartsau to present a message to His Majesty in which the provisional government declared to him their resolve to change the form of government. The king listened to the reading of the message standing erect, very pale, and with tears in his eyes.

"Gentlemen," he said at last, "it seems that Hungary hates me very much?"

"No, sir, but she wishes to control her destiny herself."

Charles answered sadly:

"I have been unable to realize anything of all to continue the war. I have witnessed the ruin of prosperity, the wellbeing of my people, and I had to continue the war. I have witnessed the ruin and crumbling away of everything. Is the fate of Louis XVI and of Nicholas II reserved for me? Or shall I be flung out from the doors of my country like a simple malefactor?"

Later he added: "Tell Count Karolyi that I shall recognize the decision taken by my country, whatever it may be. I do not wish to be an obstacle to my people's good, if my disappearance is to assure their happiness."

Four days later, on Saturday, November 16th, the republic was proclaimed at Budapest. During the morning the Chamber of Deputies and that of the magnates held their last sitting. They were gloomy sessions. A few voices were raised in timid adieus to the fallen regime. In neither of the two assemblies which Tisza had dominated by his authority during more than twenty years was a single word of regret heard in remembrance of him. Less courageous than their chief, the greater part of his partisans had abstained from appearing there, perhaps fearing that they might share his fate. After a few vague speeches, the deputies and magnates gathered together their papers and their private property from their desks and the cloak rooms. Cabs that were waiting in the street carried it all away.

In the afternoon, the provincial councils, who had substituted themselves everywhere for the regional authorities, assembled in the same Parliament House. Forty thousand people, with flags and banners, were gathered round the new building on the banks of the Danube, which had been constructed on the model of Westminster, the Hungarian architects being curiously and quite unreasonably enamored of the medieval style. Officers and soldiers on one side, priests and pastors on the other, formed two separate groups. Above the silent crowd, which seemed mournful and colorless, a keen little wind fluttered the red banners and flags, on which the chrysanthemums were already beginning to fade. At last Michel Karolyi appeared under the gothic porch. Near him was Marton de Lovaszy, conspicuous by his great height, Bouza Barna, who was very small, Garami, the Abbé Hock, Jaszi, Diener Denes, Szende, Count Batthyany, Böhm, Bokanyi, Bela Lindner, Kunfi—all the principal members of the National Council. Karolyi endeavored to speak, but his voice could not be heard. After the great seigneur came Bokanyi, the workmen's delegate. He was poorly clad and held his soft felt hat in his right hand; his rugged head, still covered with thick black hair and adorned with a heavy moustache, was lit up in the crude daylight. In a voice accustomed to dominate public meetings, he began to speak:

"Citizens—"

At that word the crowd, as though fascinated, made a step forward, with a hoarse "Ah," that sounded like a cry of joy, and then a wild clamor broke out, by which the people acknowledged that their deep desire for liberty was now fulfilled. When Bokanyi had finished his harangue,

Karolyi, with upraised hand, was the first to swear fidelity to the popular republic. The other ministers imitated him. Then thousands of arms were uplifted in the same sacramental gesture which is so often reproduced in our prints of the French Revolution. To complete the resemblance with the scenes which were enacted in old days in France, the archduke Joseph, the *homo regius,* the king's man, was seen renouncing all his titles and even his name of Hapsburg and swearing fidelity to the National Council, his hands laid in those of the Abbé Hock.

VII

— KAROLYI'S TRIUMPH —

In the general rejoicings which took place in Budapest over their reconquered independence, the citizens forgot their military disaster and abandoned themselves to the wildest illusions as to the fate the Allies had in store for them. There exists a strong feeling at the bottom of even the simplest Magyar peasant's heart which represents his nation to him, with all its different races, as an indestructible body endowed with a vitality which makes it superior to all strokes of destiny. That is the Hungarian fatherland, a living organism, firmly bound together in every part, of which it would be impossible to abstract any portion without the rest perishing. What would become of the plains, without the wood, the iron, and the charcoal from the mountains? What would become of the mountains if they were deprived of the corn and fruits of the plain? Although they are mostly illiterate, this peasant people have a far more vivid idea of their history than many a more educated nation. The popular songs which everyone there knows by heart continually represent the past to their imagination as a most glorious one, and it is due to them that so deep a longing for the liberty of those old days has been maintained. After three centuries that ancient dream of independence was suddenly realized! Hungary had at last succeeded in liberating herself from Austria! How was it possible to believe that just at that very moment the crown of St. Stephen was to be broken up? Rumor ran: "It was the fear of the Russians which threw us into the arms of Germany. From henceforward that danger no longer exists. Nothing now prevents us from returning to our old love for France. The fact that we remained firmly attached to our Allies only proves our fidelity to our promises. We have always hated Germany and there has never been in the soul of a Magyar peasant the least animosity towards the French. Today we are laying down our arms before our forces are destroyed or our territories invaded. Of our own free will we have ceased to be belligerents and have become neutrals. Therefore we must be treated as equals and not as a vanquished foe. The Entente made war on a Hungary of the past that was subservient to German policy against her own will. That Hungary is now quite dead. Freed from Austria and mistress of her own destinies, she aspires to become a democratic state like France or England. Let those liberal nations receive us, and let the West protect us, who have so long defended the Western lands!"

I have lived long enough among them to be convinced that these opinions were sincere, at least in the country districts and among the great mass of the peasants. The German is as profoundly detested there as the Austrian, and both are confused in the same contemptuous term of Nemet.[5] France, on the contrary, has left on their imaginations the remembrance of long struggles engaged in side by side. France also appeals to the peasants on account of the liberal ideas which she has spread abroad in the world, and which they themselves defended with arms in their hands in 1848. But if it is correct to say that there never was any hatred of the French or sympathy for the

---

[5] In speaking of these "Nemets" it is said in Hungary that "bacon is not made of dogs." Bismarck, when he traveled through the Puszta, was so struck by the abusive tone adopted towards his country in so many of the Hungarian popular songs that he despaired for a time of ever bringing the Magyars into line with Berlin.

Germans in the hearts of the Hungarian peasantry, how could the journalists and politicians, who for fifty years had passionately supported the German policy, dare to invoke this popular sentiment and further give strength to it by clearly expressing the thoughts which among the lower classes were still entirely incoherent? How could they forget that for fifty years the aristocracy, the financiers, the leaders of industry and commerce, all that was really of any account in the country, had submitted themselves body and soul to Berlin? How were they so blind as not to see that the Entente itself was no longer free, that it had entered into engagements with other states who, despite especially difficult circumstances, had ranged themselves by its side, and that the hour had now come for the Entente to redeem its promises? Finally, could they claim to have created a unity of sentiment in their country and to have caused the hearts of all the races which inhabit it to beat as one? Were all these diverse people as convinced as the Magyars of the indestructibility of millennial Hungary? Would not the Serbians, Romanians, Ruthenians, and Slovaks, claim for themselves that very independence for which the Hungarians were so enthusiastic today, and thus use the moment of victory to emancipate themselves in their turn?

Certainly these objections could not have escaped the attention of the journalists of Pest. But by suddenly appearing to be as madly in favor of the Entente as only yesterday they had been servile in their attitude towards Berlin, I imagine they expected to deceive the Allies, or if that were not possible, arouse against the Entente the irresistible rancor of disappointed hope. As to Michel Karolyi, by dint of repeating to himself and those around him, that he was a *persona grata* in England, America, and France, his vain and puerile mind had doubtless ended by believing it. It was almost with lightheartedness that his compatriots, inflamed by the press and their own illusions, saw him depart for Belgrade, where he was to discuss the armistice conditions with General Franchet d'Esperey.

He had chosen as his escort on this journey men whose characters he thought would favorably impress a republican general. The socialist Bokanyi and Captain Cszerniak, delegates of the Workmen and Soldiers' Council, were to symbolize the pacific and revolutionary nature of new Hungary. Oscar Jaszi represented the good will of the new government towards the nationalities. Louis Hatvany was to serve as a representative of that European spirit of which the National Council were so proud. Karolyi himself endeavored to express his democratic sentiments by a simple and easy costume, consisting of lounge jacket and sporting breeches. A few technical councilors accompanied the mission.

In the evening, when they left their hotel to go to the house where Franchet d'Esperey had appointed to meet them, they were so sure of a good reception that they expected to be kept to dinner. It is an illuminating detail that each of them had a few postcards in his pocket, which he meant to get signed at dessert.

The interview, however, was not in the least what they had expected. They were shown into a room badly lit by two oil lamps. The general came in dressed in a country suit, followed by his chief of staff and a Serbian colonel. He saluted the envoys by a slight inclination of his head, and, standing in front of the fireplace, his first words were: "The light is bad here; it is your fault. You have cut off the electricity everywhere."

Karolyi presented the minister Jaszi and Baron Hatvany to him, then the socialist Bokanyi; and when it came to Cszerniak, the Soviet delegate of the soldiers: "Ah!" said the general, "have you already come to this?"

Karolyi then read a long memorandum which he had prepared and in which he expressed the sentiments of the new Hungary which had been born in the October Revolution. "For the first time," he said "our country can put before the Entente its real will. This war has been the work of the Austro-Hungarian monarchy, which was feudal and autocratic, and which, in concert with Prussian militarism, has put Europe in flames. The fallen regime had paralyzed the strength of all those of my countrymen who disapproved of the war and who were struggling for democracy and national liberty. The Hungary of Louis Kossuth was completely muzzled. The only voices that were heard were those of the great seigneurs, whose fealty was sworn to German imperialism, and who were the declared adversaries of the nationalities. The revolution which has broken out at Budapest has changed all that. Today we appear before you, not as the ministers of the king, but as the plenipotentiaries of the Hungarian people—" ("Excuse me," the general interrupted, "of the Magyar people.") "We solemnly declare that we accept no responsibility for the political actions, internal or external, of the late government. We are not feudal lords or serfs; we are democrats, and we intend to establish universal suffrage immediately and distribute the land to those who cultivate it. We are pacifists, resolutely hostile to the old German alliance and enthusiastic partisans of the League of Nations. . . . Since the first of November we have ceased to be your enemies and have become neutrals. . . . Persuade the Poles and the Czecho-Slovaks to let the coal which is indispensable to us pass through from their countries. Save us from violence, and if you do enter Hungary, allow only the French and English, Italians, or Americans to penetrate there. Spare us the presence of Romanian, Czech, or Serbian troops, and also that of your colonial soldiers! Finally, general, we entreat you to support, by your moral influence, the Hungarian popular government in its heavy task. It is proclaiming in unmistakable accents its profound desire for peace, its democratic sentiments, and the right of nations to dispose freely of their own destiny."

Still standing in front of the fireplace, General Franchet d'Esperey replied: "Thokoly, Rakoczi, Kossuth, the great Hungarian heroes who fought against Germany, those are the names that every Frenchman respects. France has never ceased to extend her sympathy to the nation that they symbolize. But since 1867, Hungary has allowed herself to be duped by the Germans. She has become the accomplice of their rapacity. She will share the fate of Germany. You have marched with her; you must be punished with her. Your country will expiate and pay for her fault. Unfortunately it is those of the humbler classes who will suffer most from the miseries of invasion, for the rich can always leave the country. . . . You said just now that you spoke in the name of the Hungarian people. You represent the Magyar race only. I know your history. You have oppressed people who were not of your own blood. At the present moment the Czechs, the Romanians, and the Yugoslavs are against you. I hold these people in my hand . . . I have only to make a sign and you will be destroyed. Do you think that France can forget the way in which your newspapers have insulted her?"

"Not all," interrupted Jaszi, "only the nationalist organs."

"Enough, enough, I know what I am saying," the general continued. "You have come too late. Even a fortnight ago your neutrality might have been of some use to me. It can no longer help me, now that I am at Belgrade. I treat with you because Count Michel Karolyi is at the head of your deputation. We have learned during the war to recognize in him an honest man. In Hungary's present critical situation, he is the only one who can soften your fate. Rally round him."

Upon this, the general invited Karolyi and Jaszi to follow him into his cabinet. He gave them the text of his conditions of armistice, and, leaving them to a tête-à-tête with his chief of staff, his aide-de-camp, and the Serbian colonel, he went off to dine.

The armistice, which the general had rapidly drafted as soon as the intention of the Hungarians to negotiate had become known to him, had in his view the object of at once putting out of action the army with which Mackensen was still occupying Romania and Transylvania. It would also place the Hungarian railways at the disposal of the Allies, so that his divisions might be brought to Budapest and to Vienna, and if necessary to Berlin. This convention, which had been elaborated with the Serbian general staff, laid down precisely which territories were to be occupied by King Peter's soldiers and the quantity of materials, provisions, and cattle to be delivered to the Serbians had been carefully provided for. The text, however, which had been agreed upon in Belgrade, did not satisfy the Romanians. Through a singular misconception of the role of a general-in-chief, our government had not made the commander of the eastern armies acquainted with the treaty which had been made between France and Romania in 1916, and the line traced by Franchet d'Esperey modified the existing frontier but slightly. This would arouse an instant protest from the Romanians, who were anxious to enter into possession of Transylvania immediately. Also the general, who did not know the intentions of the Entente with regard to the Czecho-Slovaks, had arranged nothing on that frontier.

These shortcomings, however, would not have signified much if, as the general imagined, the armistice had been entirely a provisional measure, merely designed to facilitate a new grouping of his armies. The Supreme Council, however, gave orders that the Allied troops should not cross the Danube. The Belgrade Convention therefore remained during many months the only guide for regulating the respective positions of the Magyars and their neighbors, and its defects were obvious when it became necessary to adapt this military agreement to circumstances which were quite different to those for which it had been intended. Benign as they were, and leaving the Hungarian territory almost intact, the conditions imposed by General Franchet d'Esperey appeared entirely excessive to the Hungarian delegates. "We shall be hanged," they said, "if we accept these terms!" They returned to Budapest with the feeling that they had been received, as Louis Hatvany expressed it, not as the representatives of a civilized nation, but as envoys from an African tribe.

Despite the friendly words which Franchet d'Esperey had addressed to him personally, the blow was a hard one for Karolyi. He tried to save his face by saying that one must not be too much astonished by Franchet's want of consideration, because he was a Breton, that is to say he belonged to an "under-race" of France, which was rather an ingenious excuse for men who were accustomed to establish a severe hierarchy among the different races that inhabit their country. He persuaded his countrymen to accept the armistice by throwing out the suggestion that in virtue of President Wilsons's principles, the definite peace proposals would be less severe. Already, in his conversation, an idea began to make its appearance which was soon to take possession of his mind: "We shall always be able to get out of this trouble with the aid of a little Bolshevism!"

A new disillusionment followed quickly on the Belgrade disappointment. For centuries past what is now called the problem of nationalities did not exist in Hungary. The inhabitants were all warriors, and if a man fought well, no matter to what race he belonged, he was given a grant of lands and a title which gave him the full rights of nobility. Several of the greatest families in Hungary are of Slav, Romanian, or even Turkish origin, as, for instance, the Banffi. But towards 1830 the effervescence of a revolutionary time, the development of national thought and literature, and, above all, the policy of Vienna, which found it was to its advantage to set the diverse races of the empire against one another, aroused enmities between them which were previously unknown, and the effect of which made itself felt in 1848. Jelacsic's Croats, Kara-Georgevitch's Serbian bands, and the insurgent Romanian peasants powerfully assisted Austria to repress Hungary's efforts to gain her independence. Despite their resentment, the liberal generation to which the Kossuths, Szechenyis, and Deaks belonged, abstained from all violence and laid it down as a principle that without a good understanding among all her people Hungary would cease to exist.

The generation which followed them showed much less wisdom. Unexpectedly—but Jews always go to extremes!—Hungary developed an excessive nationalism under the influence of the Semitic press, which sowed dissension among peoples who had been long accustomed to living in fairly good harmony. It is true that the Magyar chauvinism never displayed the brutality which, for instance, disgraced the Prussian regime in Poland. Never was a Serbian or Romanian child beaten in Hungary because it had dared to say its prayers in its mother tongue! It was rather an explosion of puerile vanity which expressed itself chiefly in cafe gossip, articles in the newspapers, and in flights of oratory. And yet, though the word oppression may be too strong a one to use in connection with the Magyars' attitude towards the different nationalities in their country, one must recognize that they certainly did not treat them as equals. They did nothing or hardly anything toward their material, intellectual, or moral development. Their fault lay in a superb indifference in regard to this matter. As someone said of them, in picturesque language, "the non-Magyar people were not forced to travel on foot, they were put in the third-class carriages."

The Hungarians, who had deluded themselves with regard to the intentions of the Allies, had also been too optimistic as to the loyalty of the people whom they had so much neglected. The autonomy within the Hungarian state, which they were promised today, no longer satisfied them. The day after the Armistice, the Transylvanian Romanians formed a National Committee and claimed their independence. Oscar Jaszi went at once to Arad to confer with the Romanian delegates. He tried in vain to persuade them to remain faithful to Hungary and to form part of a kind of Eastern Switzerland. They would not hear of it. Then he also made use of the Bolshevist menace.

"Take care," said he, "for peace lies no longer in the hands of Foch and the other generals of the Entente, who as we have just experienced in Belgrade are in no way different to men like Hindenburg and Ludendorff. Peace will be the work of the European Republic of Soviets. The promises made by certain powers to the Czech imperialists and others will be held of no account by that republic. Comrade Rakowski has just been accredited to Budapest by Moscow. Men such as he will dictate the peace terms and not the imperialists."

How far was Jaszi sincere and how far was he using a diplomatic feint in the above words? Personally, communism was repugnant to this radical bourgeois; but in the downfall of all his illusions with regard to the Entente and the loyalty of the other nationalities, for that which had happened in Transylvania was happening at the same time with the Ruthenians, the Slovaks, and the Serbians, he too caught a glimpse, as a forlorn hope, of such an upheaval of the whole of Central Europe that there would soon remain neither conquerors nor conquered.[6]

Meanwhile "jacqueries" broke out almost everywhere in the country districts, as with us in 1793. The peasants took the word republic, which was so foreign to their thought, literally. It means "communal society" in Hungarian. They therefore appropriated the lands, pillaged or burnt the castles, and the rancor between people of different races was added to the tragedy of these social convulsions. In the villages also there were the old scores against the Jews and lawyers to he paid off. Murdering the Jews and wreaking vengeance on the lawyers had been the

---

[6] Only one nationality held firmly to the Magyar side: the Germans of Hungary, who were specially numerous at Budapest and in the western part of the country. They not only always declared for Hungarian unity, but even reproached the Saxons of Transylvania with having acted treacherously when they formed a National Council and announced their adherence to President Wilson's principles.

great topics discussed in letters and conversations in the homelands and at the front during the past four years. They had seen too much of the smug Jew and of his works, both in Budapest and elsewhere. Either he was ensconced in the administration, or else he traveled about the country in a beautiful uniform to make purchases for the army! Nor did they forgive those little country Jews, whose fortunes were so rapidly acquired by mysterious methods, whose wiliness was more than a match for the simple cunning of the peasant. As to the lawyers in Hungary, they play about the same role in the villages as the maires do in France: it was they who made the requisitions during the war. Now in every part of the world a requisition is always regarded by the peasant as an injustice. One must have lived in the country in Hungary to have any idea of the fury of a Magyar, who, in consequence of the zeal of a lawyer or the rapacity of a Jew, suffers the humiliation of being able to harness only one horse to his cart instead of two! The provincial gendarmerie, which not long before was a strong and well-organized body, as was natural in a country continually menaced by racial disturbances, had been disbanded. The Jews and lawyers had fallen upon evil times. The whole country was a prey to local tragedies.

There was no longer any wood or any coal at Budapest. The mines and the forests were in the hands of the Czechs, the Romanians, and the Serbians, who held up all the traffic. One after another the industries in the suburbs were closed, throwing thousands out of work. Light and heat were lacking, a double cause for sorrow and a double misery in that severe Central European winter. Famine was also threatening, for on account of the lack of fuel, only one train a day arrived in the town.

During this time, despite the armistice on all the frontiers, the Czech, Serbian, and Romanian troops were advancing into Hungarian territory, either summoned by their blood brothers or imposing themselves by force.

There was only the shadow of an army to resist this invasion. When Karolyi came into power, he gave the order that arms should be laid down on all the fronts. Colonel Lindner, his war minister, who was a brave soldier but soured by four years of campaigning, declared to his assembled officers when they came to swear fidelity to the new government: "We thought that the ideal for which we were fighting was worthy of the sacrifices which we made. I, your responsible minister, tell you it was false. A new, victorious life has been born under the star of pacifism. In future I do not wish to see a single soldier." Immediately all the men who had any sort of employment anywhere—a little holding in the country, or simply parents or relations whom they had not seen for a long time—hastened to obey this surprising colonel, forsaking their regiments, where soon no one remained but a few poor devils without hearth or home who found it very convenient to draw their pay and rations without doing anything in return.

Alarmed by the excessive pacifism of his minister of war, Karolyi dismissed him. But he himself experienced the destructive influences by which he was surrounded; he took resolutions which were quite as strange. A few troops returned from the front in good order, with their officers and arms, after having passed safely through the German, Slovene, and Ruthenian barrages, which cut off stragglers as they passed. When they arrived at Budapest, Karolyi disarmed them. More than that, he wrote to the Army Corps at Lemberg, Cracow, and Gratz, asking them to disarm every Hungarian soldier returning to his country. In this way he lost both effectives and material, leaving Hungary defenseless against the enterprises of her impatient neighbors.

There was indeed an inter-Allied mission at Budapest, whose business it was to see that the armistice was respected. Lieutenant Colonel Vix, the French officer who presided over it, did all he could to maintain the line fixed by Franchet d'Esperey. The Czechs, however, had obtained the authorization of the Supreme Council to occupy Slovakia and to advance along the Danube to within a hundred kilometers of Pest. This breach of the agreement, which he was charged to carry out, made the colonel's position a very delicate one towards the Hungarians when he had occasion to reproach them with the infringement of any of the seventeen points of the Belgrade Convention. The Romanians, who were as eager as the Czechs to take possession of the territories allotted to them by the Treaty of 1916, advanced into Transylvania and endeavored to procure there the provisions, cattle, and all sorts of materials of which they stood sorely in need after the pillaging of their own country by Mackensen's armies. With great impartiality, the head of the military mission inflicted fines upon the Hungarians when he found them in the wrong, such fines to be paid in cartridges, which were forwarded to the Poles; and he sent note upon note to the Serbians, the Czechs, or the Romanians if he heard that they had advanced beyond their prescribed limits. They, however, replied by other notes intended to prove their innocence. How could all these scraps of paper stay the irresistible advance of victorious soldiers, anxious to realize their conquest?

The precarious accord of the various parties that had rallied round Karolyi hardly two months before, and which had made the success of the Revolution of October, was already only a memory. Every detail became a cause of strife between the bourgeois and socialistic ministers. In this feudal Hungary, where three quarters of the land belongs to a few hundred great seigneurial landowners, everyone was agreed on the necessity for agrarian reform; but while the bourgeois ministers would have liked to create a class of conservative small proprietors, as in France, the socialist ministers desired to place the exploitation of the great domains in the hands of the peasant associations. The bourgeois ministers maintained openly a few regiments of officers who had organized themselves voluntarily to replace the absent police and gendarmerie; but the socialist ministers, yielding to the demands of the soldiers, organized as Soviets, clamored for their dismissal. The bourgeois ministers required that severe measures should be taken against the incipient Bolshevism, which was favored by the prevailing misery and the propaganda of the first prisoners returned from Russia; but the socialist ministers refused to enter into a conflict with people whose ideal they shared, though they might still differ from them as to the means by which it should be realized, especially because they relied on the menace of communism to assist them in their efforts to impose their program of social transformation upon the nation.

In all countries a bourgeoisie which has neither an army nor police at its disposal is a powerless class. This was particularly the case in Hungary, where it formed an insignificant minority, the major part of which was Jewish, and it was far from possessing the instincts to resistance which belong to our Western bourgeoisies. The socialists, on the contrary, grouped in syndicates to the number of about two hundred thousand, represented the only power existing in Budapest in the midst of the general disorganization. Karolyi was drawn towards them by natural sympathy. He gave the order to disband the regiments of officers, recognized Bolshevism as a political party, and declared that no one could be proceeded against for entertaining communistic opinions; he gave his adherence to the project for socializing the land, the banks, and the great industries. In short, one after another he abandoned his war minister, his minister for agriculture, and his minister of the interior, and when he was reproached for yielding everything to the socialists, he replied, as if he were a chauffeur infatuated by speed, "I have taken my place in an express train. Let those who do not wish to follow me at that pace get out."

The bourgeois ministers did get out. In order to form a new government and place the man who still remained the symbol of the October Revolution above all parties, the National Council hurriedly nominated Count Michel Karolyi president of the provisional republic, without even awaiting the meeting of a constituent assembly, the election of which the disturbed state of the country rendered impossible. Karolyi replaced the bourgeois ministers who had resigned by socialist ministers. He installed himself in the palace at Buda in the king's place. His childish dreams had come true.

VIII

— BELA KUN —

A round head which was completely bald, large pointed ears, eyes that were big and piercing, a short nose, enormous lips, a wide mouth, no chin, the whole physiognomy resembling a lizard—such is the portrait of Bela Kun. He was a small Jewish employee, clearheaded and crafty, like so many thousand others in Budapest.

Before the war he was an obscure journalist who might have been seen now and again in editors' offices, making the most trivial reports; then he disappeared. We find him again in the country, at Koloszvar, where he was performing the duties of secretary to a workmen's mutual benefit society. Accused of having misappropriated a small sum from the fund, his comrades had turned him out from his confidential post and were about to take proceedings against him when the war broke out. He went with his regiment to the Carpathians, where, in the course of the year 1916, he was made prisoner. He was sent to Siberia, to the detention camp at Tomsk. He learned Russian, and sometime after Kerensky's revolution he became a friend of the famous propagandist Radek, whose real name was Zobelsohn, now a great personage in the Ministry for Foreign Affairs at Moscow, and who was at that time employed to make Bolshevist propaganda among the prisoners. Bela Kun founded, in conjunction with another Jew who called himself Ernest Por, a weekly review, *The International Socialist*. It was published in Hungarian, and he was given a subsidy of twenty thousand rubles for it. A little later, when the German armies had penetrated far into Russia and seemed to be a menace to the Soviet government, Kun proposed to form an international battalion among the prisoners, for the organization of which he received another thirty thousand rubles. Only thirty volunteers responded to his appeal, and twenty-two of them decamped the moment they had received their bounty of 150 rubles. Bela Kun and Ernest Por marched to the frontier with the remaining eight, but at the end of three days they returned to Petrograd.

There, Bela Kun rapidly became one of Lenin's familiars. In 1918 he founded the Prisoners of War Congress at Moscow and received forty-six thousand rubles for the general expenses. Once again, however, his accounts seem to have been incorrect, for in a full meeting of the congress his comrades accused him of being a swindler.

It was at this congress that a vote was passed to establish a course of lectures for agitators. The course was to last for four weeks; each student was to receive fifty rubles a day and his food. Bela Kun and Perlstein took complete control of this teaching, which Lenin considered to be of capital importance. Successively they founded a Hungarian group, a Romanian group, with Pascariu at its head, a French group under Captain Sadoul, Czech, German, and Finnish groups, etc., to each of which Bela Kun forwarded a subsidy of sixty thousand rubles. At the same time he busied himself with the Federation of Foreign Communistic Troops, of which he was the president, and which had for its object the recruiting of soldiers for the Red Army.

I do not know whether to attribute Bela Kun's success to his powers of oratory (which were of a mediocre order) or only to the desire which these poor wretches had of obtaining for themselves, in their misery, rather more bearable conditions of life. It is certain, however, that of all the prisoners the Magyars were those who entered the service of the Red Army most willingly. It is even said that on several occasions the Hungarian Bolshevists saved the Soviet regime when it was in a critical condition.

A few weeks after Karolyi's revolution, Bela Kun, under the name of Major Sebestyen, returned to Budapest with a group of doctors and hospital attendants. On his departure from Russia he had received a sum of three hundred thousand rubles with which to begin the Communist agitation in Hungary. The Russian Red Cross in Vienna was to furnish him with money in accordance with his wants. He has himself avowed that between November 1918 and March 1919, when the dictatorship of the proletariat was established in Hungary, he received twelve million rubles.

At first his success was poor. His newspaper, *Vörös Ujsag*, the "*Red Journal*," amused more than it terrified peaceable people by violent utterances such as the following: "It is not sufficient to kill the bourgeoisie, they must also torn in pieces." The meetings in which he set forth the methods of the Russian Revolution, and which were held in strict privacy, only attracted a few "intellectuals," students of both sexes, who were for the most part Jews. The workmen's syndicates were frankly hostile to him. Even among the soldiers, with whom the regime of the Soviets and the confidential men had already been substituted for the ancient hierarchy, he was badly received, as was proved by the blundering enterprise of the January 1st, 1919.

That day, at the head of a band of about six hundred individuals, composed of men out of work, demobilized soldiers, escaped convicts, and Russian prisoners, he invaded a barrack yard and harangued the soldiers, who had come to the windows full of curiosity. Fromf one messroom a shot was fired. That gave the signal for a somewhat lively fusillade between the soldiers and the Communists. Bela Kun then abandoned the place and betook himself to another barracks, where his reception was even more deplorable. The soldiers shut him up in the guard room. His partisans tried in vain to force the entrance to the barracks. It was only through the intervention of his coreligionist, Dr. Joseph Pogany, that he was set at liberty.

This Pogany, who had assumed the title of President of the Soldiers' Soviet, was the same person who, on the night of October 30th, had led the little band that had assassinated Count Tisza. He was the son of a man who held the office of washer of corpses at a synagogue at Pest. He had studied at the university and received the degree of doctor. This was a fact which never ceased to surprise people when they saw his butcher-like appearance and his brutal face, in which two dull eyes could hardly be seen amidst the fat. Smitten with the desire for success as a dramatic author, he had written a piece (which had everywhere been refused) entitled *Napoleon*, in which be portrayed a pacifist emperor who cherished idyllic dreams of a country life in his heart, but who was always forced to make war by a malignant fate. He resembled those strolling players who, having once played the part of the Little Corporal in a theater, continue to imagine in real life that they are the emperor. Doctor Joseph Pogany, his left hand in his waistcoat and his right behind his back, his eyes puckered up as if he were looking through an imaginary telescope at the Austerlitz charges, posed as a replica of his hero; and in editors' offices his Jewish comrades laughingly pointed him out to one another as the Napoleon of the Ghetto.

When war broke out, he managed in some way to get exempted from military service—this fanatic of the god of battles only wished to imitate the great emperor in his character as a little dapper bourgeois. He was then collaborating in the socialistic journal, *Nepszava*. Every big daily newspaper at Budapest was authorized by the war minister to retain the number of editors which were considered indispensable. The chief editor of *Nepszava* did not, however, consider Pogany's services indispensable. He fell back on a paper which was of a moderate and bourgeois tendency. Thanks to Count Tisza, he was authorized to remain on the staff of *Az Est* ("The Evening"). During the whole war be distinguished himself by the ardor of his verbal patriotism and the civility which he displayed towards the meanest sublieutenant whenever by chance he went to the front as a reporter. His comrades still remember a certain toast which he pronounced when General Böhm Ermoli, execrated by the Hungarians for singling them out in preference to the Austrians to send them to their death, passed through Budapest. No journalist in Pest could be found to make a speech in his honor, but Pogany undertook the duty.

At the moment of the debacle he was quite as ready to insult the officers as he had previously been to shower adulation upon them. The same bizarre instinct which caused him to make himself an abject caricature of Napoleon drew him irresistibly towards the persons and things belonging to the army. It was to please the soldiers, by satisfying their old grudge against the former prime minister, that he took upon himself Tisza's assassination with the same zeal as that with which he had sung Böhm Ermoli's praises. That crime had given him a kind of shameful prestige, and Karolyi's government showed him simultaneously their gratitude and their disgust for having delivered them from their most redoubtable adversary.

A fortnight after the fiasco which had taken place at the Maria Theresa barracks, Bela obtained his first great success in the mining district of Salgotaryan, on the borders of the Carpathians, where he had some relations. Excited by his harangues, the working population pillaged the town for three days. On his return to Budapest he carried off his little troop of unemployed men and demobilized soldiers to attack the printing offices of two newspapers. Here again he had a complete success; all the machines were broken.

Karolyi then asked the chief of the military mission to send a few French regiments to Budapest to keep order in the town. Lieutenant Colonel Vix, who had recently had a stone thrown into his carriage, replied by inviting Karolyi to arrest Bela Kun. "Pray do us the service of arresting him yourself," replied Count Karolyi. To this the colonel objected that he was not charged with policing the town.

A few days later the president of the Hungarian Republic was forced to take the energetic measures to which he had hitherto hesitated to resort.

The unemployed, as they dispersed after one of their meetings, were suddenly moved to attack the offices of the *Nepszava*, the organ of the Social Democratic party. Karolyi, with the support of Garami, who was minister of commerce, also manager of the journal in question, called out the police. It was a real battle. Eight policemen were killed and more were wounded. In vain Bela Kun protested that he had taken no part in the fray, and that the whole responsibility rested on the shoulders of the chief of the Syndicate of Unemployed Workmen. He was, notwithstanding, imprisoned and so roughly handled by the police, who were anxious to avenge their comrades, that he had to be taken to hospital. On the following day several thousand workmen, carrying copies of the outraged journal on their hats and on the banners of their associations, organized a mass demonstration against the Communists, whom they denounced as irresponsible liars and blackguards. In the Jewish press, however, Bela Kun was represented as a martyr, a new Christ; and even within the government, two Jewish ministers, who were known to have Bolshevist leanings, energetically took up the defense of their coreligionist who had been mishandled by the police. In the same way one may see every day on the Galician frontier some Hungarian Jew, noticing that one of his brother Israelites from Poland, who had arrived without any official papers, was in the hands of the gendarmes, would fly to his rescue and save him by a pious lie: "I know him, he is my relation, my guest. Set him at liberty, I will take him home with me."

One of these Bolshevik members of the government was the minister for war, William Böhm, formerly a representative of a firm for manufacturing sewing machines, and one of the principal heads of the Metallurgist Syndicate; the other was Sigismund Kunfi, minister for public instruction. Dr. Sigismund Kunfi, whose real name was Kunstädter, had abjured Judaism in favor of the Protestant religion as being more likely to assist his university career. He taught for some years in the Lycée at Temesvar, but having attached himself to the Socialist party, Count Apponyi, minister of public instruction, laid him under the necessity of choosing between employment at a university and his political ideas. With great éclat he gave in his resignation and went to Budapest to swell the number of Jewish journalists with which the town already teemed. His mind and culture raised him high above this mediocre level, but the unhealthy fear of appearing to be engulfed in the small bourgeois ideas in which he had been brought up forced him towards extreme opinions. The mere thought of feeling himself behind any man, or a laggard with regard to any new ideas, was unbearable to him. His face was not unrefined, but his eyes squinted and they always appeared to look both ways at once, as if in fear that someone might have overreached him. Despite this, he enjoyed life, and it was remarked that of all the ministers he was the one who more than any other would throw himself back in his automobile with an air of fatuous self-satisfaction.

Böhm and Kunfi went to visit Bela Kun and the other incarcerated Communist leaders in their place of arrest. Laszlo, Korvin-Klein, Rabinovitz, etc., were among the number, all Jews. They caused their friends to be appointed directors of the prison so that the prisoners presently found themselves in fact the masters. They could communicate freely with their friends outside and assumed in their so-called dungeons the airs of heroes in misfortune, so dear to the popular imagination. The printers and compositors, the syndicates of the bricklayers and of the metal workers, and two thousand workmen who were employed in the munition factories of Csepel, in the suburbs of Pest, formed themselves into soviets. Joseph Pogany continued his propaganda in the barracks, drove out the officers from the quarters they occupied there, and decided that in future the regiments should choose their own chiefs. Soldiers could be seen strolling about the town with red ribbons and a death's head in their caps. Enormous crowds of unemployed perambulated the town singing revolutionary songs. Communistic pamphlets were openly distributed in the streets and on the tramways. The antisemitic students were expelled from the hall, where they were holding a meeting, and obliged to pass between two files of sailors, who slapped their faces if they did not take off their hats. Finally, to counterbalance the arrest of Bela Kun and his companions, the government ordered that the houses of all persons suspected of counterrevolutionary opinions should be searched, and a general and a bishop were thrown into prison.

During this time the Romanian, Serbian, and Czecho-Slovak troops continued to penetrate into Hungarian territory. Karolyi made lively representation to Lieutenant Colonel Vix that if this invasion continued it would render the triumph of Bolshevism inevitable, by forcing the Magyar patriots into counsels of despair. But the French general staff at Belgrade, instead of sending regiments to Budapest to reestablish order, recalled the detachment of Moroccan spahis who had arrived some weeks before to stop Mackensen's march, and who were in barracks there. Almost at the same moment, Vix received orders to communicate to the president of the Hungarian Republic a note from the Supreme Council authorizing the Romanians to advance about a hundred kilometers into

Hungary.[7]

Without going so far as to believe that this decision of the Entente would let loose Bolshevism, the colonel felt that it was inopportune. He hesitated to transmit the message and tried to gain time by parleying with Belgrade. He begged that at least the task of communicating to the Hungarians so serious a modification of the treaty which he was charged to carry out might be given to someone else. Meanwhile, his procrastinating phrases gave little consolation to the president of the Hungarian Republic. Karolyi was reduced to gazing at the sky from the top of his palace at Buda to see whether he could not discern signs of an approaching universal cataclysm in which Hungary might find some chance of salvation. A young Jew whom he had sent on a mission to Berne kept this kind of messianic hope alive in his imagination. He was called Kéri, his real name being Krammer. He was not an old freak like Diener Dénes nor a grotesque villain like Pogany. He was of the type so common in Israel, possessed of a spurious talent which dazzles the eyes as on entering a cinema. One of the companions of his youth, who for long was infatuated by him, has told me of certain striking traits. Oppressed by the fact that his origin left much to be desired (he was a Jew, the son of a dealer in grease and oil), Kéri circulated a story that his grandmother had been the mistress of the great Magyar poet, Pétöfi, who fell at Segesvar in the War of Independence, and that the blood of this hero flowed in his veins. He also took pleasure in boasting that he was a prey to monstrous vices and degrading perversities. This was not indeed purely imaginary. It seemed as if he could not approach a beautiful woman, or even one who was merely well dressed, without insulting her. In his eyes the need of money justified the worst meannesses. He borrowed mon-

---

[7] Besides this, the note created a vast neutral zone 166 miles long and forty miles broad, into which the Romanian and Hungarian soldiers were forbidden to penetrate.

ey of everyone: from people he had known for only five minutes, from the waiters at the cafes, and from the boys at the newspaper offices. Still, he was a fairly well-educated man with a taste for romance, which had made him choose for his abode the ruins of the old convent hidden away on St. Margaret's Island, which is one of the pleasantest places in Pest and associated with the memory of the sainted queen of Hungary. A supreme nonchalance seemed to him the indispensable mark of a great mind, and one of his pleasures was to keep the editor of his paper in an agony by the lateness with which he would send in his copy. An insolent tone, and the satisfaction of contradicting and of displeasing those around him, characterized the literary dandy whom he was endeavoring to represent. For instance, he would praise the Teutons to the skies, but if the man to whom he was talking had the unfortunate idea of agreeing with his opinion, he at once changed his point of view and depicted Germany as a country given over to platitudes, thickheadedness, and brutality. At one time he would drag the reputations of the aristocratic Magyars through the mud, at another he would vaunt their refined elegance, which he said had preserved for the world the gems of most precious rottenness. In all these babblings—whether spoken or written—he had a curious gift of deforming and rendering coarse everything upon which he touched and of imparting to things in general a passionate thrill, at the will of his most insincere imagination, which seemed to his ingenuous public an interesting effect of nature and of art.

Such a man was well calculated to dazzle Karolyi. For a long time Kéri had hung about the naive and lavish magnate in the hope of drawing some money from him. At last he succeeded in getting himself appointed to a well-paid mission at Berne. Superbly dressed, lodged in the best hotel, he led the life of the great seigneur of his dreams, in company with a good number of his coreligionists. This called forth the remark from a magnate: "Today the Jews live like counts, and the counts like Jews." In order to justify his mission and to preserve the illusory ideas of his patron, he addressed to him truculent and fanciful reports upon the European situation in general and upon France in particular. In a brilliant but inane manner, he showed him the whirlwinds of Bolshevism involving the whole world in its mad dance: he entertained his mind with apocalyptical mirages, which owed their origin to the smoke of a good cigar or the fumes of an excellent dinner. When he was at the end of inventions and arguments, he had recourse to the following decisive words: "It is a fact established by history. . . ." a formula which entered so often into his talk that his friends would accost him with the phrase, which had passed into a standing joke.

Kéri returned to Budapest on March 12th, and his conversation, even more than his letters, served to convince Karolyi that a spark would suffice to put Europe in flames, and that he himself, like a new Attila, wielding as he did the menace of the Bolshevist scourge, held the fate of the whole West in his hands. At the same time, a rumor became current that a Russian Army was advancing on the Carpathians to assist Hungarian Communism. A memorandum from Colonel Strömfeld, future commander of the Red Army, presented these rumors to Karolyi as authentic facts and these phantom Russians as a force that nothing could withstand. These rumors had their humorous side, for the Russian Bolshevists were at the same time spreading the news among their starving population that the Magyars were advancing towards Russia, driving before them immense herds of swine with which to revictual the country!

At this precise moment Colonel Vix received orders to present without delay, under the form of an ultimatum to be executed in ten days, the famous note as to the consequences of which he was so apprehensive, and which he had so much desired to delay yet a little longer. The order was categorical; he could only obey it. On March 20th, therefore, he went to the royal palace at Buda to present his message to the president of the Hungarian Republic. The moment he had read it, Karolyi convoked the attendance of the other ministers in the presence of Colonel Vix to ask their advice. They declared unanimously that they could not take it upon themselves to accept conditions which involved a peace unacceptable to their country. Some of them even (Böhm in particular) expressed themselves so violently that the colonel was obliged to tell them that he was there to present an order, not to enter upon a discussion. He retired, leaving the president and his ministers to their deliberations. What, then, were the feelings of Michel Karolyi? Undoubtedly, a profound despair seized upon him when he saw his last hope vanish of preserving for Hungary the ancient boundaries which had been hers for a thousand years. Certainly, also, he felt personal animosity towards the Allies, who, he said, had betrayed him and made him a very poor return for the separate peace and voluntary disarmament of his country for which he was responsible.

I do not, however, think that it is wronging the psychology of the man to imagine that, in the general confusion, he experienced a kind of drunken delight at finding himself confronted with one of those unexpected, tragic events which, as he had once said in talking with Countess Teleki, made for him the whole zest of life. The Entente was deserting him. He would show them then what he, on his side, could do against them, by letting loose on the world a flood of Bolshevism which would break up the whole of Europe. Those are his own words. There was in him the fury of the Hungarian peasant of the fable, who, standing on the threshold of his house, saw a storm of hail break over his vineyard and destroy all hopes of harvest. Silent and calm in appearance, he surveyed the tempest. Then when the storm was over, he murmured, "Now see, good God, what I also can do!" He took his hatchet and, going out, rushed to his vineyard, struck blows blindly to right and to left, and in a few minutes wrought havoc upon all that the storm had left. Karolyi also exclaimed, "Now Europe shall see what I can do." He reached for his axe, that is to say he let Bela Kun and his friends out of prison, gave over the power to them, and so destroyed, like a demented man, all that was left of Hungary.

The Jews, however, who up to this moment had supported him (for in feudal Hungary it is necessary to have a great magnate's name even to lead a revolution), did not even allow him the bitter satisfaction of behaving like the Hungarian peasant. The Bolshevist Revolution of March 20th, like the previous one October 30th, which had brought him to power, took place almost without his aid, and this time again it was due to the initiative of a handful of audacious Israelites. During the day, all the ministers had resigned, some because they did not wish to sign their names to a paper which dismembered Hungary, others because they felt that the hour of triumph had come for the ideas for which they had secretly worked so long. Certain now of carrying with them, by the force of popular indignation, the mass of Socialist workmen who up till now had been recalcitrant, Böhm and Kunfi sought out Bela Kun in his prison and agreed with him upon the final measures necessary for the establishment of the Soviet Republic at Budapest. All night the military motors which were at Pogany's disposal scoured the suburbs to convoke members of the workmen's and soldiers' soviets. In the morning this assembly proclaimed the dictatorship of the Hungarian proletariat. Immediately afterwards Kunfi and Kéri left the meeting and went to take the news to Karolyi and demand his resignation. But when the moment came for laying down the power which he had so much desired, the ambitious magnate hesitated. For a moment Kunfi even feared that he would make his way to the council and try to persuade the Soviets to reverse the decision they had already taken. Then, in his peremptory tone, Kéri pointed out to Karolyi that the whole town had gone over to Bolshevism and that he must leave the place. One seems to hear Kéri's speeches—his favorite phrase: "It is an established fact. All history teaches us. . . ." What joy for Kéri to have it in his power thus to humiliate a great seigneur from whom only yesterday he was asking favors! Stunned, if not convinced, Karolyi finally replied, "Well, do as you please." The two men passed into the next room and drew up the following proclamation:

> To the Hungarian People.
>
> The government has resigned. Those who up till now have held the power by the will of the people and the support of the proletariat consider that events require a new line of conduct. Production can only be assured if the proletariat takes over the management of affairs. The economic situation is critical; the external situation is no less so. The Paris Peace Conference has secretly decided to establish a military occupation of practically the whole of Hungary. The Allied military mission has declared that from today the line of demarcation is to be considered as a political frontier.[8] The object of this occupation evidently is to make our country into a strategic base against the armies of the Russian Soviets who are fighting on the Romanian front. The territory which is being taken from us is to be the reward of the Romanian and Czech troops with whose aid they wish to break the efforts of the revolution.
>
> I, provisional president of the Republic of the Hungarian People, appeal to the proletariats of the world against this decision of the Paris Conference and ask for aid and justice. I resign and place the power in the hands of the proletariat of the people of Hungary.

---

[8] This assertion was false. It was categorically denied by Colonel Vix.

When they had finished drawing up this manifesto, Kéri and Kunfi returned to Karolyi. He had with him his two special secretaries, Simonyi and Oscar Gellert, both of them Jews. Whether it was due to the nonchalance of a great seigneur, or on account of a conscientious scruple, or a supreme regret for his loss of power, Karolyi did not himself put his signature at the foot of the document. Simonyi signed it for him. It was these four Jews who put an end to the Hungarian Republic and stifled the last efforts of Karolyi's ambition.

Hardly had Kéri and Kunfi left the palace when the former president of the Hungarian Republic wished to withdraw his resignation. It was too late! Events had marched quickly. His proclamation was already known to the Soviets, and had been communicated to the whole world by wireless.

An hour later, Bela Kun and his companions left their prison in triumph.

It was only on the following day (for no papers had been published for forty-eight hours) that the population of Budapest learned what had happened. On every wall, red placards announced Karolyi's resignation and the dictatorship of the proletariat. Other placards decreed a state of siege, forbade the people to assemble together, and ordered the immediate closing of all shops in order that an inventory might be taken of the contents. Excepted were those which sold foodstuffs or tobacco, also stationers, chemists, druggists, and dealers in surgical requisites. Other notices prohibited the sale of alcohol. Like the invariable refrain of a song came the penalty for disobeying all these orders—the death penalty, execution on the spot.

Stupefied by this revolution, which had been accomplished more rapidly even than the first one, and made more anxious by it, the passersby stopped for a moment, read the placards, and passed quickly on without exchanging comments with one another. Only in front of the banks and public buildings a few Red Guards, who had nothing military about them but a rifle and an armlet, gave the streets a somewhat curious appearance. Already the conductors of the tramways called you "Comrade," which sounded particularly strange in a country where the respect for rank and title is, so to speak, inborn, and where, even the day before, you would have been called "Monseigneur," or at least "Excellency" if you knew how to be a little arrogant and dispense liberal tips.

Passing in one short quarter of an hour from prison to the government of the state, Bela Kun and his friends installed an Executive Council in the place of the former cabinet. The members of this council took the name of commissaries of the people. Bela Kun conferred the presidency of it upon Alexander Garbaï, an entirely obscure personage, but who had, in Bela's eyes, the advantage of being a Christian and so masking the Semitic character of this Communist movement. Of twenty-six commissaries, eighteen were Jews: an unwarrantable number, if one considers that there are only 1.5 million Jews among the twenty million inhabitants of Hungary. These eighteen men took the direction of the Bolshevist government into their own hands; the others were mere figureheads. It was said jokingly at Budapest that they only appeared at the Council of the Jewish Republic to carry on its business on the sacred Sabbath day, and were thus like the Christian servants in Jewish households from Friday to Saturday, do the work there which the law of Moses forbids the Jews to do themselves. Bela Kun had contented himself with the title of commissary for foreign affairs—a piece of sharp practice which deceived no one. After the dynasty of Arpad, after St. Stephen and his sons, after the Anjous, the Hunyadis, and the Hapsburgs, there was a king of Israel in Hungary today.

IX

— THE NEW JERUSALEM —

Impassioned speeches with a mystic tendency announced to Hungary that the reign of happiness had begun. "Humanity," cried the Bolshevist orators, "has never had a more splendid duty before it than now. Never was so daring an effort as ours made to overthrow all the principles by which men have lived up till now. Oh! it is good to be alive in this tempestuous epoch, when we enter as pioneers into unexplored regions. We have burnt all the bridges. Forward, always forward! Nothing must remain of the old world. No half measures, no clemency. The only question is whether we shall have sufficient strength, courage, and willpower to throw all useless sentiment overboard. Yes, comrades, we shall find the required energy when we remember our childhood, our insanitary houses, our sordid misery, and our joyless youth. It is audacity and confidence which we require! Let one passion alone animate us, love of the revolution!"

So spoke the new prophets without, however, dwelling on the fact that the sovereign proletariat was still too feeble to stand alone: it required masters, guardians, good men and true, who would lead it to its happiness in their way, in spite of itself if necessary. They set to work.

The ideal course, no doubt, would have been to decapitate at one fell swoop all aristocrats and bourgeois, but as there were many difficulties in the way of so radical an operation, they had to content themselves with making life insupportable to them.

They decreed that no one could take part in any election without a card of membership of a workmen's syndicate. This disfranchised and outlawed all the bourgeoisie with one stroke of the pen. Their deposits at the banks were confiscated, and they were summoned to pour into the state chests, within two weeks' time, all their gold and jewels, their *objets d'art*, and the whole of their foreign securities. Later on, they were obliged to give up even their linen and clothes and were only permitted to keep for themselves three shirts, a few pairs of stockings, and a pair of shoes. In their houses and apartments, they were only allowed to occupy one room or two, leaving the rest for unknown people who came and installed themselves there. A controller was appointed for each house, for whose election only the proletariat tenants of the house might vote, and who combined the duties of policeman and concierge, turning out or installing whoever he thought fit, peremptorily deciding all difficulties between the new tenants and the old, and collecting the rents on behalf of the state. He also estimated the necessities of each, distributed the vouchers indispensable to procure whatever might be required in the shops of the town, and held a perpetual menace before the eyes of all the inhabitants, of denouncing them to the Soviet tribunals.

From the first days of this regime, all the stocks of the shopkeepers had been declared communal goods, and Soviet controllers were installed behind the counters at the side of the tradesmen. A low price was fixed for each article on sale, but in order to prevent anyone who was not of the proletariat class profiting by this special price, it was specified also that no one should have the right of buying the smallest object if he were not the holder of a syndical card and of a permit given him by his concierge. Women of the highest society became grooms in riding schools or worked in cinemas so that they might obtain these precious cards, without which it was impossible to live. But, in a few days' time, nobody received anything at all, the shops having been rapidly emptied; and the despoiled shopkeepers were not so foolish as to restock them even if they had had the means.

Then, following Lenin's example, a terror was organized. "Comrades," cried Napoleon Pogany, "we will send to the bourgeoisie of this place, in a voice which will resound far, the following message: let them know that from today we take them as hostages. Let them know that they need not rejoice if the armies of the Entente make progress, for all advance on the part of the Serbs and Romanians will entail cruel experiences for them. Let them make no demonstrations, let them display no white flags at their windows, or we will dye them red with their own blood!" So spoke the son of the washer of corpses. Special troops were employed to prove that these speeches were not vain words. The chief of these terrorist bands was a certain Cserny, of pure Magyar race, a former worker in leather and a man of athletic build. He had first served in the Austro-Hungarian navy, but after a mutiny of sailors at Cattaro, he was sent to a regiment of Hussars on the Carpathian front. He conducted himself there with great bravery but was taken prisoner in the course of the third year of the war and sent to Siberia. He succeeded in escaping and returned to Budapest in the autumn of 1918, just in time to assist in Karolyi's revolution. He at once became head of the naval deserters who were in the town, and by his energy and especially by virtue of the ascendancy which his herculean strength gave him, he soon exercised complete domination over them.

Bela Kun, when he returned from Russia, got in touch with him and furnished the necessary subsidies for supporting his men. He then sent him to Moscow to study terrorist organization. Cserny returned in a very short time, having been initiated in the right methods, and bringing with him eighty professional executioners for the further instruction of the Hungarians. A Russian Jew, Boris Grunblatt, and a Serbian burglar, Azeriovitch by name, were told off to recruit men for him in Budapest. He only accepted dark-faced and dark-haired men in his band, as he found the fair ones were too sensitive. The recruits bound themselves by oath to execute in cold blood any sentence of death they might be ordered to carry out. Hanging, which requires a special knack, was, however, reserved for a few privileged ones.

The troop grew rapidly. From two hundred ruffians, which it numbered at the beginning, it rose rapidly to seven hundred. They lived for the most part in quarters in the Batthyany Palace, which came to be called Lenin's Barracks, from whence came the name of *Lenin-fiuk*, (i.e., Lenin's boys), which they gave themselves. They were clothed in leather from head to foot—leather caps, leather waistcoats, leather breeches, leather gaiters, a rifle on their shoulders, a Browning pistol and a pigsticking knife in their belts. When they went on a mission, they added to this martial array bombs which they carried in their hands. Day and night, riding on motor lorries, they scoured the town, entered houses, visited apartments, arrested the suspects denounced by the concierges, and carried off the hostages picked out by the Political Investigation Department, which sat in the Parliament House. The Batthyany Palace soon became too small to contain them all: some installed themselves in the Hunyadi Palace and some chose the Normal Institute for Schoolmasters as their habitation. Guns, mitrailleuses, and armored cars defended the approaches to these barracks, which were real fortresses of Hungarian Communism.

The Political Investigation Department had at its head a Christian workman, Guzi, but its real chief was a certain Otto Klein, who had changed his name for that of Corvin, one of the most illustrious in Hungary. From whence did he come, this little hunch-backed, scrofulous Jew, who, when he interrogated his victims, amused himself by ramming a ruler down their throats? From what underworld had he emerged into the light? No one at Budapest has ever been able to enlighten me on this matter.

In the cellars of the Parliament House, Klein-Corvin and his people carried on their work—if one can so call it—as well as in the Batthyany Palace and at the Institute for Schoolmasters. They murdered men, they hanged them, they flogged them with horsewhips or with wet cords, they put out an eye with the point of a knife or cut slits in people's stomachs; while outside, in front of the ventilators, an acolyte kept a motor horn constantly blowing to drown the cries of the victims. I have received numberless reports on all these atrocities, and it is very difficult to select the true from the false and to discern to what extent hatred and fear have added their wild imaginings to a reality already sufficiently horrible. Here, however, is a little bundle of absolutely authentic facts which may serve to give an idea of the atmosphere in which the people of Budapest lived for four months.

On Easter Sunday, a young lieutenant, Dobsa by name, was walking on the Corso when two of Lenin's boys demanded his papers of identity. He had mislaid them. At the Batthyany Palace, Dobsa enquired of the porter where he could replace them. He referred him to a Jewish functionary called Schön, who began to abuse him and call him a rogue. The ensign, his heels together in the military attitude, smiled, as with a nervous gesture he struck his riding boots with his cane. "That smile will freeze on your lips," Schön said to him, and he telephoned to Cserny: "I will send you a young fellow whom it would be desirable to dispatch to *gaides*." *Gaides*, in the Yiddish jargon, is a corruption of the Greek word hades; to send anyone to gaides meant sending him to hell. Thereupon Dobsa was taken before Cserny, who sent him back to Schön for further information. Schön sent him back again with the simple note, "Expedite him, English fashion." This was sufficient for Cserny. Some of Lenin's boys dragged the lieutenant to the cellar and, showing him a great pile of coal, told him to dig his grave in it. He resisted. They hailed blows on him. The unfortunate boy began to dig with his hands. When the hole was large enough, his executioners made him fall into it by firing a bullet into the back of his neck. Then his body was thrown into the Danube. For many days after that, a woman might have been seen in the neighborhood of the Batthyany Palace, enquiring for the young lieutenant, who she thought was a prisoner there: it was Dobsa's mother.

M. Hollan and his son, the one a former undersecretary for state, the other a railway director, were denounced by their concierge as being suspected of anti-Bolshevist tendencies, and their names appeared on the list of hostages drawn up by the sinister Otto Klein-Corvin. One night a motor lorry, driven by Red Guards, drew up at their door. "I am going to make it hot for these two," declared a certain Andre Lazar, who was directing the expedition, and for whom the elder Hollan had once refused to sign a request asking that he should be dispensed from military service. The terrorists went into the Hollans' house, arrested them, and forced them into the motor.

Then the lorry, continuing to sweep up its victims as it went, took up a secretary of state, a judge of the Assize Court, and some members of the Court of Cassation, who were all thrown into the bottom of the car. It was freezing hard that night. For a moment, Lenin's boys considered whether it would not be more charitable to kill these people outright rather than let them perish of cold. But Lazar objected that Cserny would be displeased if they returned empty-handed. They therefore agreed that they would only lighten the lorry of one of its passengers. Whom should they choose? First they thought of the president of the Court of Cassation, but Lazar voted for the Hollans. He stopped the car at the entrance to the suspension bridge which connects Buda and Pest, and, getting down himself, with a secret agent and four of the Red Guards, he forced the Hollans to alight also. The little party walked towards the steep bank of the Danube, which was at that time encumbered with masts and poles brought by boat to be used for the decoration of the town, for the first of May was approaching. This made it very difficult to get to the edge of the water. The prisoners were brought back to the bridge, and when they reached the first pier, Lazar ordered the Hollans to turn their faces to the Danube. He placed himself behind the son and a Red Guard behind the father, and they shot them both down with their revolvers. The Red Guards took the bodies by the head and feet, balanced them on the parapet, and threw them into the river. Then, smoking and laughing, they all rejoined the lorry which was waiting for them at the other end of the bridge.

Three gendarmerie officers had been denounced by one of their subordinates as suspects of conspiring towards a counterrevolution. Cserny had them arrested. For days he tried to draw a confession from them. Finally at the end of its patience, the Tribunal condemned them to death, and asked the Lenin-fiuk on duty in the hall which of them would undertake their execution. Five offered themselves at once. It was about midnight. After having suffered nameless tortures and outrages, the three officers were hanged on the pipe of the heating apparatus which went across the cellar. Having done this, the executioners called through the ventilator to the chauffeur of their lorry, inviting him to see the sight. The man came in. The others showed him their work, saying, "You would not have dared to do that?" Upon this, without answering, he climbed a ladder and slapped the face of one of the hanged men.

Enough of these atrocious stories, which could be multiplied indefinitely, if it were not superfluous, after the three examples which we have given, to show by further facts whither the bestiality of man during a time of revolution may lead.

All the workshops employing more than ten workmen

had been socialized. The directors and engineers could keep their place in them if they accepted the new order of things, and in that case they received a maximum salary of three thousand crowns a month. It was, however, understood that on the day when the Communist regime should have attained perfection, they would not be paid any more than the other comrades. The profits, of course, were to go the state—but there were none. Prices became fabulous, and to cite only one example, a twenty-heller piece cost double its nominal value to make. Soon the commissaries of the people had themselves to acknowledge that their methods did not bring the returns they expected. "When I examine the results," declared the commissary Varga, at a sitting of the Economic Council, "I am obliged to state that they could not be worse. So far as the mines are concerned, the output has diminished by one half. In industrial undertakings, the losses are from thirty to sixty percent. When I look for the cause of this, I find that it lies not only in the lack of coal and raw material, but also in the slackness of the work of the individual. Under the capitalist regime, if a workman did not accomplish what was expected of him, he was quite simply sent away. We have renounced this brutal method; another conception of work is in process of formation but is slow in establishing itself.

When will the proletariat understand that without assiduous work they will be unable to satisfy their wants? Meanwhile we are forced to revert to the system of reducing the wages of those who do not accomplish their task." In the last days of Bolshevism, production had fallen so low that, in order to raise it a little, they returned to the plan of paying the workmen not by the day or the hour even, but by the piece and according to the work which they had actually done. It was in effect reestablishing the old system of wages, which they had wished to suppress.

They had similar experiences in financial matters. At first some resources were obtained by seizing the money and securities in the banks, selling the stocks of merchandise which filled the shops, and confiscating the goods of the church. This money, however, melted away very quickly in paying exorbitant salaries and in maintaining the enormous number of Soviet functionaries that had grown up as if by a miracle from one day to another. (It is, in fact, a fatality which attaches to all regimes which make their appeal to the conscience of the workers—that they have to employ an infinite multitude of controllers, and thus rapidly create a new privileged class far more numerous and sterile than the old bourgeoisie). The rest of the funds were employed in supporting the Communist propaganda in Austria, Romania, and Czecho-Slovakia, and especially in Germany, where Bela Kun subsidized the riots at Hamburg and the revolution in Munich. Besides this, there was much robbery and malversation, and large sums, the amount of which it is difficult to estimate, were placed in safety by the prudent "friends of the people" in Geneva or Zurich to provide for the bad time which they foresaw. The treasure chests were soon empty. Then a humorous state of things came about. Two months had hardly elapsed since the establishment of the dictatorship of the proletariat when the Soviet government, which treated the bourgeois as parasites and exploiters, invited these same bourgeois to place any gold or securities that might remain to them in the banks, and promised them eight per cent interest on all they might deposit, double what they had previously received!

In their extreme embarrassment, the Soviet government thought very naturally of issuing notes. But the printing presses and the blue paper with the watermark of the Austro-Hungarian bank were in the mint in Vienna. They were therefore forced to make use of any sort of white paper and to have recourse to ordinary printing presses. This white money, as it was called to distinguish it from the blue money, became the official currency, and under the most severe penalties the people who still possessed blue notes were forced to exchange them with the least possible delay for the new ones. It was hoped in this way to get back into the state chests notes which, however depreciated they might be, were still the only ones that were worth anything abroad. It was vain for the Soviets to boast that they gave as security for their paper money not the worthless guarantee of metallic reserve, but the resources and work of the whole nation; no one was duped. It was too painfully clear that their badly exploited resources had become nonexistent, and everybody closed his purse.

Even intellectual activity, in its most spontaneous expressions of art and literature, was socialized. The state exercised its control over all the productions of the mind by means of censors chosen from among the writers and changed once every six months. Representatives of the Soviets watched over this committee in their turn, for "it is a well-known fact," declared a commissary of the fine arts, "that successful writers are infallibly inclined to conservative ideas." Intellectual creations were divided into two categories. The first comprised all the works which were accepted, printed, and spread abroad by the Soviet government because they propagated their principles. The second was composed of works which were simply intended to satisfy the public taste. The writers of the first kind received the maximum salary awarded to specialist workmen. As to the authors of books which aspired only to please, they worked at their own risk and peril. It was the worse for them if their works met with no success; but if they had a great sale, the profit which they could receive for them must not in any case exceed the maximum price fixed by the government for its volumes or propaganda. This, the moralists explained, was done in order not to encourage a mercantile spirit in literature.

In reality things worked out rather differently. First there was the group of friends, those of whom the commissaries were sure and who received brilliant monthly salaries, without anything being demanded of them—a mark of respect for genius, which could not be forced to produce. Then there was the group of those who produced at the command of the state and who did furnish something, and naturally received rather less. Then there were the real artists (and they were the best in Hungary) whose works could not fail to be hostile to the new ideas. They received the lowest salaries of all, coupled with the condition that they should cease to write or paint.

Theaters, cinematographs, pleasure resorts became free. It was only necessary to show the syndicate card to obtain admittance. A special commission arranged the repertoire, and at the end of every performance a lecturer expatiated on the benefits of the new era. As no one ever stayed to hear him, however, it became necessary to place his discourse in the entr'acte.

Most of the Christian professors had been expelled from the university. They were replaced by young Jews, many of whom had only just passed their examinations. The faculties of law and theology which were, of course, of no further use, were suppressed. As for the system of examinations, it was abolished because it entailed inequalities which were quite incompatible with the modern spirit. The teachers and professors of the schools and colleges had to attend a four weeks course of Bolshevist instruction, after which the comrade instructors (as they were now called) were authorized to resume their functions. In each school a committee composed of ten of the pupils watched over the purity of the Communist teaching, proposed the necessary changes to the Soviet, or denounced to the tribunal, as a poisoner of the youthful mind, any master who might have pronounced imprudent words. The study of Latin and Greek had been struck out of the programs, and the classical books of the St. Stephen Society had been destroyed. There was, of course, no longer any question of religious teaching, and as the theory prevailed that the principal evils from which family life suffered were due to the ignorance in which the children were left with regard to sex relations, courses of hygiene were instituted for boys and girls, which gave rise to scandalous exhibitions, sometimes in the hospitals, sometimes in the so-called Museum of Plastic Art, and sometimes in the cinematograph. They were always accompanied by discourses on free love.

Officially, Bolshevism invariably denied that it in any way attacked the exercise of religion or interfered with liberty of conscience. The Jews of the Soviet Republic did not wish to be accused of conducting a religious war against Christianity. This was only prudent in that old-established country where Catholics, Lutherans, and Calvinists were each deeply attached to their several faiths. Kunfi, the people's commissary at the Ministry of Public Instruction, proclaimed in a decree that the Soviet government left complete liberty to everyone as regarded his creed; that the churches and other religious buildings would not be turned into cinemas, theaters, or public houses; that nothing would be changed with regard to marriages or the organization of the family, and that the republic had never had any intention of establishing community of women. Priests, pastors, and rabbis had to read this lay mandate to their faithful flocks, a fact which shows that the attitude of mind of the majority of Hungarians was averse to the new regime, and that in the eyes of the simple people, Bolshevism was suspected of a desire to ruin all that time and experience have founded on Christian thought and sentiment.

A few days had sufficed to overthrow the old established order at Budapest. A handful of people who felt neither scruples nor regrets in sacrificing a world which was completely strange to them had upset everything in order to reconstruct it in their own way. A New Jerusalem was growing up on the banks of the Danube. It emanated from Karl Marx's Jewish brain and was built by Jews upon a foundation of very ancient ideas. For centuries and centuries, despite all disasters, the Messianic dream of an ideal city, where there shall be neither rich nor poor, and where perfect justice and equality shall reign, has never ceased to haunt the Jewish imagination. In their ghettos, filled with the dust of ancient visions, the wild Jews of Galicia persist in looking out on moonlight nights to see whether, far away in the firmament, they cannot discover some sign of the coming of the Messiah. Trotsky, Bela Kun, and their followers had once more revived the fabulous dream. Only, tired of looking to Heaven for this Kingdom of God which never came, they made it descend to earth. Experience has shown that their ancient prophets were better inspired when they placed it in the clouds.

X

— IN RURAL HUNGARY —

Budapest is not Hungary; the real Hungary is the country—the great expanses of corn land and the vast pastures where flocks feed peacefully.

One can walk for miles and miles there and never come across even the smallest or most isolated house. This beautiful country, where the soil is so fertile, gives at times the impression of being almost uninhabited. It was not so formerly. In the days of the Anjous and the Hunyadis there were farms and castles and monasteries everywhere; but the Turks ravaged it all three centuries ago, and the plain became again an immense pastureland. The shepherd's reed hut took the place of the well-built farm, and large market towns grew up, in which the peasants crowded together to obtain protection from the janissaries and the spahis.

Although the Turks were driven out of Hungary more than two hundred years ago, the aspect of things has not changed much. No doubt cultivated areas have by degrees almost everywhere replaced the uncultivated steppes, but rural life never again spread itself over the fields. It remains concentrated in enormous villages, in reality rustic cities of several thousand inhabitants, which are all exactly alike. The little low, lime-washed houses, with long roofs thatched with reeds and forming deep eaves, are aligned in regular rows at right angles to the road, like the lines of a camp with deep bays. Each block of buildings only presents its gabled ends to the street, while its facades, its doors, and its windows look out upon a vast yard, which is hidden from the passerby by palisades of boards. This is evidently a reminiscence of Asia and expresses a desire to protect the intimacy of family life—a taste for secrecy common to all oriental habitations. In the middle of the village stands the church, surmounted by a cross, if the people are Catholics, or by the Gallic cock if they are Calvinists; a little apart lies the cemetery, where the graves are dotted about irregularly, here and there, under the acacia trees, with the old desire of the East to give to the dead that gift so precious to the living—leafy shade in the midst of heat. Beyond the village again, far as the eye can reach, one sees the immense, gently undulating plain, with its harvest and its pastures.

In this monotonous landscape, one thing only strikes the eye: the high pole belonging to the well, which seems like an uplifted finger, saying to men and beasts: "Approach, there is water here." There is nothing intrinsically beautiful in that species of gallows, at one end of which hangs a bucket and at the other a stone to make a counterweight. Yet the moment it appears in sight a feeling of infinite pleasure comes over one. That pole, with its stone and its wooden bucket, and the little square of planks which surrounds the shallow well over which it leans, comes from so far away! It is one of those inventions which are born with man and will not disappear until his place knows him no more. All that is most primitive and most simple in village life, as well as all that is most elevated in Magyar dreams, is centered round it. All the confused voices dispersed in that vast silence seem to obey it and to accommodate themselves to its law. It might be the baton of some musical rustic who conducts an agricultural and pastoral melody—a song limpid as that water which it draws up to the light.

Here lives a peasant, one of the salt of the earth; his faults are amiable ones and even his virtues are amusing. Proud and domineering, and full of a quiet disdain towards his alien neighbors, he is quite convinced that God in paradise talks Hungarian. He is the spirit of hospitality personified, and he would never think of asking any guest who came to him: "Who is your father?" To be well received, it is only necessary to drink deeply silent to taciturnity, even when he is drunk he preserves his dignity intact, but he will be moved to tears and bury his head in his arms on the public house table as he listens to the gypsies playing.

Whence comes the delightful saying: "The Hungarian amuses himself tearfully." Of an amorous temperament, with a poetical soul, only an Arab can vie with him in celebrating his loves in improvised verse, in songs and images drawn from the rustic life around him. He adores horses, beautiful teams harnessed with floating leather thongs and cloths embroidered with tulips and pinks. He loves amusement and dancing, squanders his possessions in mere display, runs thoughtlessly into debt, and is in no sort of hurry to pay his creditors—not because he is at all dishonest, but because he finds a great pleasure in seeing them get angry. He abhors untruthfulness and would quarrel with his nearest relative if he lied to him. His principal grievance against the Germans and the Jews is that he says they have introduced deceit into the country. Headstrong and obstinate, it is difficult to get him to admit himself to be in the wrong, but when he is once convinced he gives in with a good grace and without an afterthought. He is a grumbler at home and plays at being the morose master. He says complacently: "Money is good when it is counted and woman when she is beaten," but all the same the wife, who never addresses her husband familiarly and always calls him "my lord," manages everything in the house. Commerce is repugnant to him—he leaves it to the Jews. Excessive work does not please him either: is not

Providence there to see that the plains produce the best corn in Europe and the most luscious apricots? As to such vulgar things as vegetables, he leaves the care of them to the Bulgarian market gardeners. What suits his indolent and dreamy temperament best is the life of a shepherd.

I shall never forget the long summer days and nights that I passed with the shepherds in the midst of the rich pastures, the remains of the ancient steppes. Nothing troubled the peace of the prairie but the flight of a flock of black and white storks, or the quick, gliding motion of a band of wild ducks on the ponds of the saltwater marshes, or the slow movement of the vast herds of cattle that graze on the plain. Sometimes I stayed with the horse rangers—the guardians of those little Hungarian horses that furnished in those days (already prehistoric) nearly all the animals for our Parisian cabs. How free and gay they were in their wide pastures, before they came to us to lead a Parisian life and to kill themselves some frosty day on the slippery ice of the Rue des Martyrs! Sometimes I stay with the herdsmen among their cattle, white of hide and with gigantic horns.

There one often saw a bull who, having grown too powerful to please his brothers, had been driven out of the herd by their horns, leagued against him. He consequently lived in solitude, full of fury and rancor, filling the air with his deep-voiced bellowing and digging deep holes in the ground as he pawed it up. At other times I would go and sit among the sheep, by the side of the master shepherd, whose crook—or rather I should say his scepter—was marked all the way down the pole with a multitude of mysterious signs, which made it a register of the flock. As daylight, waned the dogs began their work; the horsemen in white linen, mounted bareback on their steeds, galloped in wide circles in pursuit of strayed animals, and the immense, docile flocks crowded together and assembled round the dead tree and the truss of straw which marked the place of their encampment. Phantomlike, a few belated storks showed up between the earth and sky, and thousands of wild birds made a tremendous babble by the mirrorlike pools of stagnant water, where the light of the last hours of the day was slowly dying. Then we all sat down round the iron pot containing the red pepper-flavored stew. An unalterable tradition fixed everyone's place. Each one dipped his fingers into the scarlet sauce and fished out the potatoes and bits of beef, and when the master shepherd thought that we had all had enough, he took a clod of earth and flung it into the pot; the remainder belonged to the dogs. Then the pipes were lit, we exchanged a few words, and there, under the stars and wrapped in their sheepskins, the shepherds slept in a peace like that which hovered over the first night of the world.

What power could the nervous excitement of a few ghetto dreamers have over this ancient peasant life? And yet the poor day laborer would not have been sorry to possess a few acres himself, and the small proprietor would also have taken pleasure in the division of the great seigneurial domains. The Communists of Pest, however, instead of dividing up the estates, exploited those immense landed properties for the benefit of the urban population. As in the past, the farmer and the agricultural laborers had to work for the benefit of others; they had only exchanged one Jew for another, as the men whom the commissaries charged with the management of the communal domains were for the most part just as the stewards of the seigneurs had been before them. Despite the high wages offered to them (a Soviet swineherd received fifteen hundred crowns a month), the peasants showed no desire to be employed on these national lands. As for the small proprietors, whose goodwill the commissaries of the people tried to gain by respecting their possessions and promising them exemption from all taxes, they suffered impatiently under the curse of the enormous wages they had to pay to their laborers and the notorious law of the eight-hour day, any infringement of which incurred a fine. They obstinately refused to sell their corn harvests at the price fixed by the Soviets; they sent neither animals nor vegetables to the market, and that year they only sowed as much as would produce a crop sufficient for their personal use. In consequence, the Hungarian towns suffered a dearth of food such as they had never experienced before, and this notwithstanding that they lay in the midst of a country incomparably rich in cattle and cereals. In the market of Budapest, one turnip cost five crowns.

In order to force the peasants to give up their produce, and especially for the purpose of suppressing the revolts which broke out here and there, a special detachment was recruited from among Lenin's boys and charged to organize a terror in the country. This detachment, which numbered about thirty individuals, had an armored train for their barracks, carrying machine guns, and were always ready to descend upon any village in which they had been warned that a riot was likely to break out. At its head was a puny, stooping, consumptive young man, with long hands in which the veins showed clearly through the skin, his face dull and bony, his eyes like those of a dead fish, with a long nose, flattened towards the tip, a large mouth and thick lips, and heavy black hair which he brushed straight back and which gave him the appearance of wearing a sealskin cap. His head was set on a long neck, on which the Adam's apple rose and fell above an impeccable collar—for the man was a dandy. His name was Tibor Szamuely.

He was one of three children of a Jewish family from Galicia that had emigrated into Hungary a short time before and had acquired some degree of affluence in one of the northern counties.

He, like Pogany, Bela Kun, and the greater number of the commissaries of the people, belonged to the category of intellectually discontented men who considered that society did not sufficiently recompense their talents He was a journalist—insufficiently educated, and with no special gift for his work—and had made his debut in a curious little town, very characteristic of Hungarian provincial life. It is worthwhile to transport ourselves thither for a moment in spirit.

Nagy Varad, "Great Varadin" as our ambassadors and military commanders of the seventeenth and eighteenth centuries call it in their official reports, is situated on the extreme limit of the Hungarian plain towards Transylvania, on the banks of a marshy river, the Pecze. It is a town of about sixty thousand inhabitants (of which twenty-five thousand are Jews), to which the agriculturists of the plain come to sell their goods, especially their wool and corn.

In the middle of it there is a vast square, on which are four large cafes that are always full. We will enter the first we come to. The house has a good appearance—it is an old building of the time of Maria Theresa, covered with a yellow limewash, and with a high-pitched roof, which gives to the whole a respectable and dignified appearance.

It is two or three o'clock in the afternoon. All the tables are occupied. The table of the gentlemen of the Hussars, the table of the infantry officers, the table of the subprefect and other high officials of the comitat, the table of the state railway officials, the table of the actors from the theater, the table of the Jewish merchants (wool, leather, corn, etc.), the table of the journalists belonging to the Catholic newspaper, the table of the Jewish journalists (who exchange their articles with one another), and finally the table of the literary men, novel writers and budding poets—for Great Varadin prides itself on its intellectual life, from which it derives its nickname of Paris on Pecze! All these people smoke, talk, play cards, do business, and discuss the questions of the day over innumerable glasses of water which accompany the coffee. Suddenly the door opens. Dressed not without care, yellow gaiters on his legs, a green hat on his head, a country squire from the neighborhood enters the cafe. At the door stands his carriage, with its small, wiry horses, neat like himself and covered with ribbons. As he passes up the room, he is greeted by the gentlemen at the Hussars' table and directs his steps towards the table of the wool merchants, to Pinkas Kohn, or Moses Loew-Hirsch.[9] The popular joke about the latter's name is that he is so rapacious that the first part of his name is always busy devouring the second. Five minutes later, after a short conversation, Pinkas Kohn, or Loew-Hirsch, may be seen drawing out of his pocket-book and counting out to the gentleman with the green hat the bank notes which he is advancing him on his next wool clip or on the harvest which is still standing. All the other guests look on. Meanwhile, the officers glance up from their cards, the Jews gaze through the smoke of their pipes or cigars, the journalists pause as they write their articles on the marble tables, the gypsy behind his violin, all follow the scene with the keenest interest, despite its being well known to them—for it is a daily occurrence. If you return there in the evening, the cafe will still be full. The infantry drink beer and the cavalry wine. The gypsy, a little tired, beats his cimbalom and scrapes his violin to some plaintive tune:

The Aspen leaf
Falls in the autumn.

Or else:

When I was a child
I also had a mother

Suddenly, about eleven o'clock, the country squire of the afternoon reappears noisily, accompanied this time by the actors and actresses from the town theater. He has paid his coachman the ten months' wages he owed him and

---

[9] Lion-deer.

also satisfied the first of his creditors whom he happened to meet, with Pinkas Kohn's money. Then he hurried to the florist and ordered a bouquet to be sent to the theatrical star of the evening, and here he is back again, escorted like Maecenas and ready to scatter Pinkas' bank notes all over the cafe. The gypsy, who was drooping, finds new ardor and strikes up his favorite song (for he knows the favorite airs of all the seigneurs of the neighborhood):

*Who has not five or six doxies
Has not an ounce of brain.*

Hungarian champagne flows in rivers. Jews and Christians fraternize in pleasant lightheartedness, when all of a sudden a sublieutenant on horseback, much exhilarated, forces his way into the room, knocking over a tray of glasses of water in his progress, and cries, brandishing his riding whip: "It smells of Jews here." But our country squire rises, bottle in hand, and approaching the gay reveler, he offers him a glass. "Drink," he says to him, "I tapped the Jew this morning." He makes the horse drink also, calls the gypsy, and empties the dregs of the bottle into his violin. The wretched man laments, "O, my lord, O divine master, O my king, (the whole Orient seems passing by), you have ruined your poor gypsy, you have spoiled his violin!" The other, pulling out his pocketbook, gives him his last bank note. Everyone there is enjoying himself—even the commercial Jews, who, a moment before, were a little alarmed. Perhaps you imagine that Pinkas Kohn secretly despises this rural spendthrift? You are entirely mistaken. This country squire is still a superior being in his eyes. Even when he is drunk, he respects him. He has been taught to bow his back to him for so many generations! That dissipated hussar represents to his eye an aristocratic elegance, an ease of manner, to which he knows that he himself personally can never hope to attain. Happily for him, he has a son at the Lycée at Budapest, and he hopes that one day the dear boy and those who come after him will have those magnificent manners, will spend their money with the same incomparable ease, and will feel no regret for it in their hearts, arousing the same respect among those around them that he himself feels for the sublieutenant and his riding whip.

It was in this atmosphere of Paris on Pecźe that Tibor Szamuely was initiated into life, aping the manners of the gentry, filling the twelve hours of the day with intellectually erotic, foolish talk (and the days are long at Great Varadin), accumulating many grudges in his mind and a thousand unsatisfied appetites, dreaming of the moment when some sudden chance should transport him from the Pecźe marshes and open up the paradise of Budapest to his ambition.

The happy moment came. He left for the capital—but he can hardly be said to have succeeded. Although it is customary there for the journalist to display a certain pseudo-elegance, his affectation of being a dandy and the care which he took to avoid his poorer confreres, with the preference he showed for making up to more fortunate people, gained him but small sympathy. Always with an eyeglass in his eye and most carefully dressed, it often happened that he had nothing to eat. On those days he stayed in bed. With the vanity so often found among the Jews, which is at the same time their strength and their bane, he represented his position as a most brilliant one in his letters to his parents; and before his companions, who, however, were not deceived, he posed as the son of a great family. All this would not have mattered if he had had real talent! But he had none, and the trick was often played upon him of pinning to the wall in the editor's room some ridiculous lines that he had written.

The difficulty he encountered in making a living obliged him to return to the provinces. He remained for several months at Fiume in the pay of the governor, which he earned by getting little paragraphs into the newspapers for him. He was, however, always obsessed by the idea of Budapest, and he reappeared there. No newspaper would make use of his services. A Catholic press agency took him on as stenographer. This did not prevent him from attending socialist gatherings, whose secrets he afterwards betrayed to the conservative newspapers.

During the first months of the war, he was attached to the official telegraph bureau, and he declared that if he were forced to go on active service be would not molder there long. He kept his word. One hour and a half after he had arrived at the front, he deserted to the enemy. He boasted of this himself.

He met Bela Kun in Russia and worked in concert with him at the communistic propaganda in the prison camps. He is accused of having got a number of Magyar officers shot because they were not sufficiently pliable. Then he came back to Hungary, and Bela Kun gave him the command of everything in the rear of the army, with a commission to repress any counterrevolutionary movements which might spring up in the provinces.

His activity was frightful. Constantly, whether by day or by night, he would get into his armored train or his red automobile, accompanied by his Lenin's boys, all armed to the teeth, and conduct a punitive expedition somewhere. It might be at Kalocsa, at Kapuvar, at Sopron, at Csorna, at Püspök-Ladany, at Czegled, or at Dunapatai, everywhere whence news was brought that the peasants had cut a telegraph wire, attacked some Red Guards, or refused to deliver up their cattle and corn. He arrived in the village surrounded by his leather-clad men, who held bombs in their hands. The peasants denounced by the local Soviets were brought one after another before this revolutionary tribunal, composed of a single judge, round whom were grouped Szamuely's companions. He himself, seated on a chair, his legs crossed carelessly one over the other, and smoking a gold-tipped cigarette, joked and laughed and was generally facetious in the following manner:

"Well, comrade, what have you done?" he asked a peasant who was trembling with fear.

"Nothing, sir, I have done nothing, the others forced me to march with them."

"Take him away," said Szamuely to two of Lenin's boys. "He is a poor wretch, I pardon him . . . do not hang him—shoot him."

One day at Kalocsa there were numerous executions. Some professors, one schoolmaster, some merchants, some officers, and a number of peasants were hanged in front of the windows of a Jesuit college. The cord broke, which suspended one of the victims, and he escaped. The recalcitrant man was recaptured and once more suspended to his branch.

Eight professional executioners made part of the thirty men who followed Szamuely everywhere. Their chief, named Arpad Kohn Kerekes, was only twenty-three years of age. He was an iron-turner by trade, and he himself acknowledged that he had shot five persons and hanged twelve; but when the day of reckoning came, the indictment accused him of one hundred and fifty assassinations. Among the other professionals there were also Louis Kovacs, Charles Strub, Isidor Bergfeld, Alexander Vigh (who hanged eight peasants at Kalocsa), Didier Reinheimer, who executed twenty-five at Debrecen, and Arthur Barabas Bratmann, who distinguished himself at Sopron. Sometimes Szamuely amused himself by tying the rope in a beautiful bow round the victim's neck; he also found pleasure in making him kiss it. He even pushed sadism so far as to force a relation of the condemned man to pull away the chair which supported the wretched victim, or he would force the schoolchildren to file past the place where his victims were dangling and would arrange for an unsuspecting woman to pass by the acacia tree from which the body of her husband was hanging, stiff in death.

Once, however, things nearly turned out badly for him. It was at Kapuvar. Followed by a few Lenin-fiuk, he entered the houses, called for the master of each, and, pointing with his finger to a tree by the side of the road, he said, "go and stand under it." Soon six men and one woman were dangling from the branches. More executions were about to follow, when, rifle in hand, brushing aside Lenin's boys, a Red Guard, who was a native of the village, advanced towards Szamuely, fixed his eyes upon him, and said, "Comrade, that is sufficient for Kapuvar today." The dark glance of the soldier made him realize that perhaps it would be dangerous to continue the game. There were no further executions at Kapuvar on that day. Each of these expeditions was coupled with the collection of cattle, poultry, wine, vegetables, and corn, which was sent off in wagons to Budapest. Then Szamuely would return to town and might be seen in the Othon, a club affected by the Jewish journalists, where formerly he had received many affronts. Now, more of a dandy than ever, his black hair thrown back, his lounge coat of irreproachable cut, clasping his hands in an absent-minded manner, he appeared to recognize no one.

XI

THE DOWNFALL OF THE SOVIETS

The first of May was a day alike of triumph and of agony at Budapest. The town seemed to be painted red from top to bottom. The order had been given to dye the old Hungarian flag red, and in every house the concierge saw to it that the tenants obeyed the order effectively. All the monuments which recalled the superannuated heroes of old Hungary—Arpad, John Hunyadi and Corvin, Thokoli, Rakoczi, Bishop Pazmany, and many others—were boxed in with boards painted red and covered with bloodred placards. In front of the Parliament House, the statue of Julius Andrassy—he who had been Bismarck's man and the tool of the Triple Alliance—was covered in by a sort of scaffolding which vaguely reminded one of a Greek temple or a "Thora" cupboard. At the foot of the statue of Saint Gerard, apostle and martyr of Hungary, an immense, glaring picture was placed depicting as in an allegory the Paradise of the Proletariat.

At one of the principal crossroads there hung four enormous globes which appeared to have been dipped in blood; they symbolized the worldwide success of the revolution. Everywhere there were busts of Karl Marx, Lenin, Trotsky, Liebknecht, and Rosa Luxemburg, who seemed, as it were, the presiding geniuses and saints of the festival. One passed under a series of triumphal arches, amid banners, five-pointed stars, and Solomon's seals, and reached, by way of Andrassy Street, the Millennium Monument which was erected twenty years before to celebrate the thousandth anniversary of the arrival of the Magyars in the country. It was hidden from view by Oriental draperies, and on the steps leading up to it was reared a colossal effigy of Karl Marx, surrounded by allegorical figures.

But all this red paint, all the processions, the triumphal arches, the fireworks, and the speeches made on this day of apotheosis could not hide the most profound anxiety. Once more the Amalekites were threatening Jerusalem! Lenin's three hundred thousand Russians, who were to save Hungary, had remained phantoms of the Oriental mirage. Instead, enemy armies were crossing the frontiers on the pretext of succoring their blood brothers who had remained on Hungarian soil and saving them from the excesses of the Communists.

The day after that glorious first of May, the Soviets learned with stupefaction that the Romanians had crossed the Theiss and that the Czechs were at Miskolcz; and already disbanded soldiers were pouring back to Budapest by road and by rail. The rumor was even rife that evening that the people's commissaries had resigned. Bela Kun, however, having been informed that the Allies disapproved of the Romanian advance, made a speech at the council, in which he said he was prepared to carry on the struggle to the end. "If we wish to fight," he said, "it will not be either to defend the integrity of our territory, or to resume on our side the policy of oppressing the nationalities. But we have a mission. We will take our part in the battle which is being waged throughout the world between capitalistic imperialism and Bolshevist socialism. We are the soldiers of the National Revolution; we must fight for the honor of the Hungarian workers and for the sacred cause of the proletariat throughout the world. So long as it is possible to fire a shot, we will not lay down our arms; we will not yield an inch of the ground of which the proletariat are masters." He concluded with these words: "It is a superstition of mine to believe that if the dictatorship of the proletariat fails here, it will be because it has not cost enough bloodshed." For those who knew how to understand this speech, it meant that the workmen must be prepared to quit the factories, the cinemas, and the streets of Budapest and rejoin the army. In the midst of rounds of applause, the assembly voted enthusiastically that at least half of the commissaries of the people and members of the council should go to the front immediately. But the commissaries and delegates of the Soviets at once forgot their oaths and stayed quietly at home.

The Red Army was reorganized in the greatest haste. Here again it was necessary to return to the old bourgeois methods, which were not at all democratic, but which had been proved efficacious. Moreover, as Bela Kun said—to justify this return to the past—"the greatest difference between yesterday and today is that yesterday we were conducting the fight from below, now we are conducting it from above. Of course the point of view changes, and what might have been wrong yesterday has become right today." The Soldiers' Councils, the election of officers by the men, political discussions and meetings in the barracks, all that had been "good" when it was wished to destroy the bourgeois army; today it was "bad" when it was a question of putting a really efficient fighting tool in the hands of the Soviet government. The cadres were reconstituted by recalling to service all the officers of the regular army; obligatory conscription replaced the system of voluntary enlistment; the merciless code which had so revolted the anti-militarists a short time before, by which mutinous soldiers were shot; the distinction of grades was reestablished, and the only novelty was that instead of stars on their collars, the officers wore braid on their sleeves and caps.

Böhm, war minister and former agent for sewing machines, and Napoleon Pogany, son of the washer of corpses, had subsided into the second place. Colonel Strömfeld, a former officer, had become the soul of the new Red Army. Of an excellent bourgeois family, a pupil at the Military School of Vienna, nothing predisposed this man towards revolutionary ideas. After the Austro-Hungarian disaster, however, he turned first towards the Socialists and then towards the Communists, hoping that his warlike spirit, which five years in the field had not satiated, might still find a useful outlet, and that he might thus satisfy what had become a real need of his nature. He was the exact type of the regular professional soldier who never fails to make his appearance whenever and wherever there may be a revolution. For a moment all Hungary placed confidence in him: the Reds because they hoped much from his strategic talents; the Whites because they counted upon him to overthrow Bela Kun. He disappointed them all—the Bolshevists, because he did not succeed in leading them to victory, and the Patriots because they had not understood that for this professional soldier the post of chief of the general staff, which had been given to him, was the goal of his ambition, and that he saw nothing beyond it.

During this time, the French troops encamped at Belgrade and in southern Hungary, looked on with piled arms while Bela Kun and his friends ruined Hungarian life, encouraged communistic hopes in the whole of Europe by their apparent success, and organized at their ease an army which they meant to launch against the Czechs and Romanians. A few battalions would have sufficed to bring to reason that regime, which was execrated by the whole population; but the Supreme Council had formally forbidden any intervention in Budapest affairs. The order was signed "Clemenceau," and it was French regiments that stood on the Hungarian frontiers. Indeed, the Magyars are inclined to put the whole responsibility on France for this inaction, which was so fatal to their country, as if the

French alone controlled the decisions of the council! The Americans, Italians, and English would not have been at all pleased to see French troops installing themselves in Budapest, and French influence imposed upon the whole of Central Europe. On this occasion, as upon many others, the French were forced to act against their own interest. The prestige which victory had given to France made it all too easily credible that her word was law in the councils of the Allies.

There was another grievance. At Szeged, an important town on the plain, on the banks of the Theiss, a few Magyar politicians had formed a counterrevolutionary government and set up a little army of about six thousand men, formed of soldiers and especially officers, who had escaped from the Bolshevists. The Hungarians bitterly accuse the French of having failed to support that government and that army. They quite forget that without French aid that government and that army could not have existed. It was French officers who went to Vienna and brought Count Teleki and his friends from their place of refuge there to place them at the head of the government of Szeged. As a matter of fact, very few magnates consented to follow them; most of these gentlemen preferred living in Vienna, at the famous Hotel Sacher, where they enjoyed excellent cooking and lost their money at cards. It was with a French safe-conduct and accompanied by a French officer that Count Teleki and a few others passed without hindrance through Bela Kun's Hungary. It was with the protection of French troops, and under the benevolent eyes of the French general staff, that they were able to organize their ministry and their army. If they had shown immediately a more decided spirit, if they had lost less time in gossiping in the cafes and in personal quarrels, if the few thousand officers who found themselves at Szeged had started to march resolutely upon Budapest, with the arms and munitions which the French had lent them, many of the peasants of the plain would have rallied to them on the way, and they might perhaps have overcome the Bolshevist forces which at that time were almost nonexistent. Instead of that, they discussed politics or amused themselves at Szeged, and they left time for the Supreme Council to declare that they did not recognize their reactionary government. The French officers found themselves obliged to take back the rifles they had so kindly lent, and for the future to maintain a more reserved attitude. The Hungarians forgot the services rendered and only remembered that the French had refused to aid them further. The legend then grew up that the French had betrayed Hungary and the failure at Szeged was attributed to them.

Meanwhile, at Budapest, Bela Kun, encouraged by some easy successes which his army had gained over the Czechs, now thought he would attack the Romanians, with the hope of rallying the whole nation around him by a military exploit. He also firmly believed that a general revolution would break out simultaneously on the same day, July 20th, in Germany, England, Italy, and France. So he chose that date to launch his offensive. But that catastrophic day, July 20th, 1919, was a most peaceable one throughout Europe. The world revolution in which Bela Kun believed as naively as Karolyi had done a short time before did not take place. And to crown his humiliation he was very soon made to realize that his soldiers were useless.

The Bolshevists had crossed the Theiss. During the first days of the encounter the Romanian Army appeared to retire before them; then, suddenly attacking them, they overcame the Soviet troops, who lost half their effectives in less than a week. The rest hurriedly recrossed the river, and the Romanians invaded Hungary, determined this time that they would accomplish the work of policing Hungary against the Bolshevists, which the Supreme Council had so imprudently refused to confide to the French.

After the sufferings of their country during the Austro-

German occupation, it was to be foreseen that the Romanians would not comport themselves with the forbearance of the soldiers from Touraine or Burgundy. Not only the Bolshevists, but the whole of Hungary was made to suffer terribly. The Magyars declare that this invasion alone cost the country as much as four years of war had done. They have never ceased to reproach the French for not having spared them this experience, while the Romanians still owe the French a certain grudge for having ultimately summoned them, in energetic terms, to abandon the territory which they had allowed them to invade.

Bela Kun had lost the game. On the afternoon of the 1st of August, he gathered together the five hundred members of the Soviet Council: "The proletarians," he cried, "have shown themselves to be unworthy of the revolution. They have betrayed the confidence we placed in them in a cowardly manner. For the moment we must yield to necessity, but I shall come back soon. We are only postponing till later the advent of the Communistic Era, when the proletariat will be better prepared to receive our ideas!" It is reported that at this point he broke down and wept. It was no longer a time for speeches or tears. The Romanians were approaching. A special train was waiting for him and his friends at the railway station. He, Pogany, Kunfi, Amburger, and the other Jewish commissaries of the people quickly took their places in it. Only Christians were members of the Socialist Ministry which took over the conduct of affairs at Budapest. Not a single Israelite had tried to obtain even the most insignificant post in it.

Bela Kun passed the frontier without molestation. He arrived in Vienna, where the government then in power, which was half Bolshevist, interned him for form's sake. A few months later he escaped and reached Germany under a false name. Just as he was about to embark at a Baltic port he was arrested by the police. The Budapest government demanded his extradition, but it was not granted. Bela Kun went to join Lenin and Trotsky at Moscow. At the moment when I write he is presiding at Odessa, with ferocious severity, over the commission which is charged with maintaining southern Russia under Bolshevist tyranny.

Corvin Klein, Arpad Kohn-Kerekes, and other Jews of less importance, who had not been admitted to Bela Kun's special train, paid with their lives for the princes of Israel who had fled to Vienna. They were tried and hanged.

With an animal unconsciousness of danger, the chief of the terrorist troops, Cserny, still walked about Budapest for a few days quite unconcernedly. Then he suddenly took fright and escaped to the country. For a week he wandered like a hunted animal in the forest of Bakony, but the gendarmes captured him, and he too was hanged. As for Tibor Szamuely, the news of the downfall of the Soviets was brought to him at the town of Győr during a nocturnal sitting of a revolutionary tribunal. He had just condemned three wretched workmen to death. He at once broke up the sitting, and, leaving the condemned men to their fate (no one dared execute them after his departure), he regained the capital. Why did he not take his place next day in Bela Kun's special train? No doubt he thought it more prudent to employ an automobile for his flight; but he was arrested at the Austrian frontier by the customs officers. Pulling a handkerchief out of his pocket, he pretended to wipe his forehead, and blew out his brains with a small revolver, which he had secreted in it. The local Israelitish community refused to receive his corpse in their cemetery. He was buried apart, and on the tombstone someone wrote in blue pencil: "Here lies a dog."

XII

— A DIALOGUE WITHOUT END —

In the cathedral at Granada, where lie the mortal remains of Isabella the Catholic, a curious panel of painted wood represents some Moors, with their high turbans on their heads and clad in the gandoura, who are crowding round a pitcher to receive baptism and thus assure their salvation in the next world, and especially in this one. Something of the same kind could be observed in Budapest in the last days of Bolshevism. Never since the faraway time when Saint Stephen the King made Christians of his barbarian followers in masses had there been so many conversions in Hungary. Horrified at the idea of the excesses which would inevitably follow the failure of the Jewish Bolshevist attempt, hundreds and hundreds of Jews rushed to be baptized. They hurried to the church, as if it were the safest insurance company in the world.

Their fears were not unfounded. The dictatorship of the proletariat had left behind it such violent hatred of the Semitic race throughout the whole nation that even today it dominates all other sentiments and surpasses the humiliation of defeat and the sorrow caused by the diminished size of the country. Israel again experienced one of those cruel moments, such as the Jews have passed through so often in the course of ages, but which in this case held an additional drop of bitterness, because they had learned to consider Hungary as their promised land. From one end of the country to the other, the people fell upon the Jews. Szamuely's crimes and those of Lenin's boys were added to all the peasants' ancient grievances against them. Still more recently, when the Romanians invaded the Hungarian territory, sweeping up all that they could carry away, the country Jews had received the invaders with the servility and spirit of opportunism which they always show by placing themselves at the disposition of the strongest; and it seemed monstrous that after they had been such strong supporters of Bolshevism, they should now side with the Romanians who had come to overthrow Bela Kun and his friends! They should be made to pay for it. Many tragic scenes were enacted in those very places where a few weeks earlier Szamuely had lorded it over the people with his band of bomb carriers. Near the town of Orgovany, I passed through a little acacia wood, light and transparent in the summer sun, where, without any shadow of formal trial, the people of the neighborhood had hanged sixty-two Bolshevists at once, the greater part of whom were Jews. A peasant who accompanied me, and who had undoubtedly taken part in the affair, said, as he showed me his hands with an enigmatic smile: "There is no blood on my fingers, but there are no more Jews in the village." Troops of officers who were without pay or professions, and who had taken upon themselves the mission of purging Hungary of Bolshevism, scoured the country, carrying out summary executions to avenge the sufferings which they or their families had endured during the communistic time and the Romanian invasion. At Budapest, some of these detachments (as these bands of officers were called) had installed themselves in several large hotels and made them their barracks. Incidents took place there which are not spoken of, and rapid and ferocious dramas were enacted—exact reproductions of the Bolshevist horrors—which only serve to disgust one with humanity altogether. As I write these lines, I have under my eyes the report of an English labor mission which worked in these parts, and which is as terrible to read as the little wood at Orgovany was horrible to walk through. Although it is very difficult to separate the true from the false, there seemed to arise from that paper the same unsavory odor of blood which sickened me among the acacia trees.

That paroxysm of fury died down gradually, but I was still able to see for myself scenes such as the following. It was evening, and I was at a cafe in Budapest—one of those cafes which is always full and where a great part of the life of the townspeople is passed. Suddenly a noise was heard of people running in the streets, of carriages driven at a great pace, and at the door there appeared officers belonging to different detachments, in various uniforms, followed by a hundred or more demonstrators, attached to the anti-Semitic league of the Awakening Hungarians or the Awakened Hungarians. A panic broke out in the cafe. Some of the guests hid under the billiard tables or the sofas, others rushed to the lavatories, others to the telephone. There they were stopped by an Awakened Hungarian who said: "It is useless to try to call the police, all the wires are cut." During this time the officers were making the round of the tables, asking everyone politely to show their identification papers. A Jew was recognized by the hasty way in which he rose from his seat even before he was addressed. He was at once seized, passed from hand to hand, and, as if by magic, was relieved of his pocketbook, his purse, his watch, and his cigar case before he reached the door. Then he was thrown to the crowd, who received him with various cries and exclamations, of which one remains in my memory: "Knock him on the head so that he may not become lame." The cafe thus purified, the inquisitors courteously saluted the remainder of the guests, took their leave, and continued their unheroic exploits elsewhere.

It happened during one of these brawls that a Jew pleaded that he had been baptized, and even exhibited his baptismal certificate.

"Very good," replied the officer, "recite the Lord's Prayer to me."

"Our Father which art in Heaven. . . ."

The new convert could get no further. He was thrown into the street among the crowd to learn the rest.

These brutal scenes no longer take place today, but the Jewish question remains. All Hungary has risen up to suppress the Jews. They wish to expel the five hundred thousand Galician Jews who arrived in the country during the war. The number of Jews admitted to the university has been limited so as to diminish their position in the liberal professions; the Masonic lodges, which had become almost completely Jewish, have been closed; everywhere Christian banks and cooperative societies are being established to replace the Hebrew middleman. Publishing houses and newspapers are being created whose mission it is to defend the national intellectuality. A violent struggle has been entered upon between two spirits and two races. Here are some of the voices, which seem to rise alternately above the daily noise of combat:

"Ah, those Jews!" exclaims the Christian, with a heat engendered by the sense of his lamentable weakness as opposed to the formidable strength of his adversary. "How they have deceived us. For more than half a century, all our statesmen, liberals and conservatives, Catholics or Protestants, have vied with each other in opening our country to them. We were so afraid that Europe would regard us as old-fashioned Turks or a retrograde people. We silenced our deep antipathy so as to appear intelligent, modern, European, or anything else you please to call it. We put a bandage over our eyes and, following the example of civilized Europe, we proudly declared that it was only barbarians who could see anything but a simple religious quarrel in the Jewish question. We remained deaf to the warnings of those who said Germany, England, or France, can allow themselves to receive the Jews with generosity if it seems good to them so to do. In all those three countries put together, with a total population of over a hundred million, the number of Jews hardly amounts to that which we have in Hungary. Germans, English, or French can pour a bottle of ink into their big lake with impunity. If we, however, pour the contents of that bottle into our Hungarian soup, we shall not longer be able to eat it. We shut our eyes to these prudent counsels. We naively believed that these thousands upon thousands of strangers could be easily assimilated and would become like ourselves. Fifteen sous was sufficient to work a miracle! For that sum they could change their names. For seven pence halfpenny, Kohn could be changed to Bela Kun, Krammer was transformed into Kéri, Otto Klein into Corvin! 'Just one Magyar more,' we would say; it was so much gain for our little nation, so lonely, so isolated on the frontiers of civilization. We would not look into their hearts; we were so foolishly satisfied to see them disguised as Magyars, talking our language, and adopting some of our customs and many of our faults. At the end of two generations these wild Galician Jews had become great personages. Thanks to the sentiment of family and race which was so strongly developed in them, they helped one another on, took possession of all the professions which were capable of assuring them fortune and power, and only left us the glorified misery of the administration, the sinecure offices, and all the inferior trades. Do you ask for figures? In prewar Hungary the Jews numbered about five percent of the population. But out of every hundred doctors, engineers, lawyers, or journalists, fifty were Jews; of every hundred merchants, fifty-six; of every hundred editors, fifty-seven; and of all employees in commerce or industry more than half were Jews. On the other hand, none were to be met with in the more arduous employments. You would hardly have found one Israelitish blacksmith, mason, or servant among a hundred workmen of that class. In the country, a quarter of the landed property had fallen into their hands, while in equity they should have possessed barely a twentieth part. You would not have discovered a single Jew among a hundred agricultural laborers. Our unfortunate nation has really- become a country of officials, squires, and peasants, dominated by an elite of Jewish financiers, merchants, and intellectuals. 'It is for the good of Hungary,' they said. For a long time we believed it ourselves. It is perhaps true if merely material progress and approximation to reputedly superior forms of Western civilization be considered progress. They have built the city of Pest, of which even yesterday we were still proud, which rises like a monstrous wart on our plain, a hideous conglomeration of all our faults and their own. They have plunged us into the current of great European affairs by developing a financial life in Hungary so intense that there is not a goose or a hen that does not lay eggs for their banks! They have even undertaken to form our mentality upon Western ideas, for thought itself is a business with them, a profitable occupation, like the exploitation of a special make of automobiles or sewing machines. They have only put before us a parody of Western civilization, just as they themselves are caricatures of Hungarians. Unconsciously their brains deform all the thoughts which lodge in them; and in all they have brought us, a true European no longer recognizes the spirit of his race. In London, Paris, and Berlin, they also corrupt everything they touch, but it does not matter, because there are people who create ideas there, and powerful indigenous forces, so that what the Jews ruin in the mill of their sensual, vain, passionate, erotic, and shallow nature, are incessantly reestablished. We here are abandoned without any such defense to their mischievous genius, to the talk which dazzles us, to their newspapers and reviews, their stage plays, their spiritual nourishment of a most inferior kind, seasoned with spices which quite destroy our taste. Can they even claim to have borne their share of the sacrifices entailed by the war? I do not mean their fair share, calculated according to their importance in the country—that would have been too much to expect—but simply their share in proportion to numbers? At first they made a great noise, shouting out their patriotic sentiments on all occasions, and, to flatter our vanity, showed themselves more Magyar than the Magyars. But when the hour came for proving their patriotism otherwise than by speeches and newspaper articles, their one care was to escape military service and retire into the background. In the recruiting committees, half the members were Jews, and they were not wanting in finding pretexts for exempting a coreligionist. In the army itself, the mass of peasants were unsuited to be secretaries or clerks, so it was natural that the Jews should settle themselves in those employments. The number of Jews killed as compared with Christians is eloquent in itself. While the Christians left a quarter of their effectives on the field of battle, only eight percent of the Jewish officers were killed. Forty-eight percent of the Christian pupils of the higher schools were killed, while only seven percent of the Jewish students perished. As for the private soldiers, seventeen percent of the Magyars and only one percent of the Jews were killed. What do these few individuals matter, when we consider the five hundred thousand emigrants from Galicia who, during the war, found a haven in Hungary? Then sir, in the moment of defeat, what did they do to show their gratitude to us for having received them so generously in their hour of need? They tried to destroy our civilization utterly, and they installed Bolshevism in our midst. The best that can be said on this score is that for some of them it represented the latest form of the Messianic idea, and for the others a brutal determination to establish the domination of Israel over all the earth."

"All that," replies the Jew, with a frightened, yet cunning air, through which we seem to catch a glimpse of Heinrich Heine's smile, "is only the contentions of jealous shopkeepers and students anxious to defend their mess of pottage. Let us look at the matter coolly. Thank God, you do not bate us as much as you pretend you do. Your aristocrats cling to us, for we do business for them. Your Catholic clergy (the higher clergy—the only one that counts—of course) regard us also with favor; we administer their estates, their confidence in us is unbounded, and besides, we afford an opening for their zeal in the matter of conversions. Your Protestant pastors are so penetrated with the biblical spirit that they cannot be really hostile to the descendants of Abraham and Moses. Be frank! Even your peasants do not hate us. Has there ever been any sign of a pogrom in Hungary. The hangings which have taken place during the last few weeks are sad accidents—artificially organized—we shall not bear them malice on that account, for at bottom the peasants were innocent in the matter. No, our true, our only enemies are your noble idlers, your timid and indolent bourgeois, who would do much better to work than to waste their time in spitting at the Jews. Christian merchants, doctors, lawyers, journalists, and students cannot forgive our success. Is that our fault? Can anyone make it a serious grievance against us that we belong to a more energetic, more subtle race than the Hungarians? Is it out fault that we are always first at school and at the university? Can we be reproached for being cleverer merchants and more daring industrials than the Christians? I have sometimes heard it said that our success is due less to our intelligence and our energy than to a certain lack of scruple. That is easily said! If I look around me, I do not see that Christian probity is very superior to Jewish probity. I will, however, concede to you that our dishonesty has more imagination and is further reaching than yours. The consequence of this is that as we obtain greater results, we attract more attention. For example: during the war I knew many poor wretches of Christians who did their best to defraud the state; they made their oxen lick salt in order that, being made very thirsty, they might be blown out with water when they were sold to the administration. A Jew works in a different way: he makes the general drink. It is just a different method that does not alter the fundamental facts. Another grievance: we are not only reputed to be the great disturbers of trade and the extortioners of the nation, but also to have a pernicious influence upon its soul and spirit. It seems that we arouse febrility, doubt, eroticism, and I know not what else; all that is morbid, impatient, and exasperating; all, in fact, that leads to the destruction of the old sentiments and thoughts that were for centuries the life of the nation. Ah, how little you know us! Is not our great fault, on the contrary, that we are so unstable, so mentally effete that we accept all too easily the thoughts and manners of other races. But, dear sir, believe me, our fathers and our grandfathers have had but one idea since they settled in Hungary. They wish that their sons should resemble them in no single particular, and that instead of leading the life they themselves have known—that of a merchant eager for gain—they should become cavaliers like the sons of the country squires from whom they purchase their corn; should fling their money about gracefully, and when they enter a cafe, should know how to ask the gypsy to play their favorite airs. It is we, alas, who have contracted all the faults of the Hungarians, as we catch all the faults of the various people with whom we sojourn for a time, and when I am told that the Jews have perverted Hungary, it seems to me one might say with greater truth the Hungarians have corrupted the Jews. In conclusion, I admit that the result is not happy for either. As for the reproach that we wished to turn all Europe upside down, which it is the fashion in the present day to throw in our faces because a quartette of Jews has upset everything in Russia, and because here also a band of fanatics has acted in a manner of which all Judaism disapproves, such an accusation seems to me to argue a very poor historic sense. There are few Jews in France, and yet I would wager anything that if France had been defeated there would also have been a new commune. Even if we were to admit that at Budapest, as at Moscow, Bolshevism was our work, what have you to say about the millions of idiots who allowed themselves to be led astray? I do not deny, however, that the revolutionary myth has always exercised an almost irresistible attraction upon us. We are a people made up of charlatans and dupes. We throw ourselves with fury into all the passing ideas, and we can be made to believe what anyone wishes. We have believed in the Law, we have believed in our prophets, we have believed in the doctors of our Talmud, in Zohar, in socialism, in all the doctrines which promised us a glorious future. We are like jackdaws that pounce greedily on anything which shines, we are poor moths that burn ourselves in the fire of ideas. I ask you, do you know any history more fertile in illusions than ours? For centuries we have waited for the Messiah, and we shall wait for him forever. We have believed in innumerable Messiahs, and the ridiculous, the fantastic thing is that the only one who presented himself humbly and seriously we crucified—for fear, I believe, lest with him we should reach the end of our dream too soon! Our Communists of today, those who call themselves the men of the future, are only the ghosts of a past which is very far away; they are the same old doctors, rabbis, prophets, and cheats. Karl Marx's *Kapital* is just the Talmud over again! But do not be deceived: the breath of revolution is not the only form of Israel's genius. The truth is that there exists in our race a singular opportunist spirit, an energy always ready to turn circumstances to account. In a well-established, sane state we are Disraeli, the greatest supporter of tradition and order; and the same desire for action and power (two indistinguishable objects) brings forth, in troublous times, a Trotsky or simply a Bela Kun."

At these words the Christian can no longer contain himself. He breaks in upon the Jew's speech with these words:

"But that is exactly what we cannot forgive! You work in all countries alike for good or evil with the sole object of satisfying the instincts which you carry in your blood. You are only interested in yourselves. You give free rein to your strength for the mere pleasure of exercising it, or rather because you are unable to put any restraint on it. You are never hampered by a multiplicity of feelings which our special and particular past has created in us, by a tradition which, though it is unconscious, is all powerful and may cause us to sacrifice our personal interests and even our lives in defense of things to which you will forever remain strangers. There are certain realities which you grasp at once with marvelous shrewdness. There are others, and they are the most important, relating to our souls, which you will never understand—any more than we can pride ourselves upon penetrating the inmost thoughts of your hearts. Our mistake for the last fifty years has been to imagine that we could make Hungarians out of Jews at will. That is impossible. The most loyal among you recognize the fact and rightly glory in it. No man can have an unlimited treasury of affection, no man can love more than one fatherland at once. You have yours; it is all the more splendid because it is an ideal one, founded on hope and situated in the clouds. Do not try to deceive us or to deceive yourselves. You can have taste, sympathy, and attachment for such and such foreign nations; you may be naturalized, baptized, and faithful to your new religion and country; it can go no further. You are Israelites and as Israelites you will remain the most nationalist among men. I do not owe you a grudge for it. On the contrary, I admire you. Every race has its mystery which sustains and preserves it. You have your secret—a magnificent and venerable one—like that of all nations. Realize that while we receive you generously in our country, we do not care to place our destinies in your hands. I willingly agree that we Hungarians are less subtle and less energetic than you. We possess but little aptitude for that modern life which you have so powerfully contributed to create in your own image. But we have an old-world, childish soul, generous and chivalrous; an old Oriental soul, indolent and dreamy; a character of our own, which has come down to us through the ages and a national temperament which has been formed by a thousand years of history. It matters little to us that, thanks to you, we might resemble the rest of Europe more closely, at all events in appearance. We wish to remain ourselves, good or bad, intelligent or stupid. We have endured your insinuating domination too long and all the false prestige which you have endeavored to foist upon us. We throw it off today. We refuse to be led, like cattle on our plain, by strange herdsmen—even though their names be Abraham or Moses."

And the Jew who, for the last two thousand years, has been accustomed to hear far more bitter words, and has managed to extricate himself from far more difficult positions, replies in his turn, without any trace of anger: "Be careful how you repeat with us the experiment which succeeded so badly when the Spaniards expelled all the Moors and Jews from Spain. That was five centuries ago, and they are still suffering from the results. Besides, it is impossible that you should seriously think of deporting us en masse, as in the days of Isabella. Neither would you wish, I take it, to fling us all into the Danube! Any exceptional measures which you may take will merely have the effect of binding us together more closely and increasing our strength. To the best or the worst among us, as you choose to regard it, to those, I mean, who had reached the last stage in the renunciation of Israel, and who no longer felt a thrill pass through them when they heard the word 'Jew' (or that dreadful word 'Israelite', which is worse because it embodies false politeness and hypocritical consideration): to those men I say, you would restore the sentiment of Hebrew nationality and rekindle the race spirit in them by persecution. For myself, only yesterday I felt nothing but disgust for all those wild Jews newly arrived from Galicia for their insensate fanaticism and their revolting dirt. I got out of the tram so as not to smell their horrible odor and not to see those dreadful types of Judaism. Now that they are being persecuted, I think of them only as my brother Jews and place myself on their side. I am not alone. I could name to you many another Jew who, during the Bolshevist regime, was disgusted by the excesses of his coreligionists and, dreading reprisals, rushed to the font; but the moment he beheld the scenes of violence which he had foreseen and the incredible insults which were heaped upon his brothers of yesterday, he denied his denial and reentered Israel. Let me tell you a secret. People say readily: "How strong these Jews must be to have maintained themselves and developed in the world despite all they have suffered." You must not say "in spite of"; it is just because of that persecution and not in spite of it that we have become what we are today. We have only produced great things when we were in misery and sorely tried. Our Bible was conceived in the time when we were only pillaging Bedouins, errant and threatened tribes. From the moment we formed a settled state our genius waned. Of Solomon's famous temple no vestige remains, but it seems it possessed more of the sumptuousness of the East than of real beauty. The Psalms of David and the Song of Solomon are the only durable monuments that we have of that time. Daniel prophesied during the reigns of the kings, but his work was not of the best. The two great voices of Israel, Isaiah and Jeremiah, are the voices of sorrow and exile. The Talmud first saw the light in the hell of Babylon. Believe me, we are not more intelligent than ordinary mortals; I think that in general our race is but a mediocre one. We lack creative originality, the power to make great inventions. We have been unhappy, and we have acquired a certain contempt for those who despised us and a disdain for the calamities which threatened to crush us, and which we overcame. It has given us a cruel and realistic view of humanity and of life, and an undoubted power of craftily frustrating the hostility by which we are surrounded. We are a salt, a tonic, a poison, what you will, in European life; we have our place in the chemistry of the world, we are a necessary element which cannot be eliminated. We have immense faults, I know them even better than you do—try to preserve yourselves from them. We have also virtues—it is for you to profit by them."

So the dispute continues between the Christian, never tired of making accusations and complaints, and the Jew, who has always fresh arguments to advance in his own defense. It is an old debate, a threadbare story, which has formed a theme of discussion in the West for so many centuries. Other subjects have lost their interest in the course of the ages; but this eternal dialogue crops up invariably from time to time, now here, now there, ever active and alive, and the dramatic part about it is that it is impossible to imagine that it should ever have an end.

XIII

— THE STAFF OF AHASUERUS —

The day I left Budapest, I saw, at a little distance from the station, long rows of railway carriages at a standstill on a siding, which presented a truly lamentable appearance. There was no varnish on the woodwork, no glass in the windows. Grass grew between the rails and rust covered the wheels, proving that the trains had been stationary there for a long time. Yet these carriages were overflowing with passengers. They were everywhere: in the compartments, in the corridors, even on the footboards; men, women, and children, talking, gesticulating, shouting, carrying on without any shame the humblest household tasks. One glance was sufficient for me to recognize that the singular occupants of this stationary convoy were Jews—these railway carriages were a ghetto.

Some of the men still wore the ancestral uniform—the caftan, the round hat and shoes down at the heels. Others had already replaced the old, weird clothes by a more modern style. But, under those overcoats which were too long, and those astonishing frockcoats which went down to their feet, I recognized the wild Jews! I found them again just as they had appeared to me long ago (ah! in what an unforgettable way), out there in their native country.

Long ago—that is to say, about twenty years since—I

had gone to the Carpathians with no other object than to look for mountain lakes and legendary castles in the midst of romantic forests, when all of a sudden I discovered a world of which neither Baedeker nor Joanne had ever told me. I can still see myself in the railway carriage which was taking me along the edge of the torrent of the 'Waag, swollen by the spring rains, on through the pine forest from which rose, right up into the sky, the snow-covered summits of the mountains, glittering in the sun. Now and then I noticed, as I passed a footpath, Slovak peasants with fur caps on their heads and dressed in sheepskins, with surprising red leggings secured by small leathern thongs; women also dressed in skins, their legs bare or covered by high boots, embroidered kerchiefs on their heads, their hair hanging in long plaits on their bosoms, and smoking long black pipes. At the little stations at which our train stopped, among the sheepskins, colored fichus, and scarlet breeches, there was a strange mixture of people clad in black, with black hats, black caftans, black and muddy boots, carrying old traveling bags, pushing one another in their efforts to climb into the railway carriages, as if it was a wheel of fortune which glided along the rails and which must be seized. They all wore untrimmed beards, which floated in the wind—long black or red beards—and an assortment of curlpapers which hung like corkscrews about their cheeks. I was also struck by the extreme mobility of their eyes, and their whole personality expressed perpetual movement and surprising promptitude. They walked with giant strides and elbows akimbo giving and receiving rude blows with them, for which they neither apologized nor reproached anyone. They were marvelously at their ease in the midst of the thaw and of the mud that bespattered their long, musty overcoats. But the most extraordinary thing of all (at least for a traveler who was comfortably established out of their reach) was the gaiety and bright joy of life which characterized that sordid crowd. I saw before me Jews from the villages buried in the mountains, the commercial delegates of all Upper Hungary—of its herdsmen and its charcoal burners, who have no idea even of what a town is like, and who rely on these extraordinary people to sell their produce and to do their commissions.

I could not get over my surprise that two such totally different kinds of human beings as these peaceful peasants, whose faces expressed nothing but rustic simplicity, and those sons of the East, whose looks and gestures proclaimed so energetic a spirit, could possibly live side by side. It added to my astonishment that the Jews appeared by their costume to belong to an even more archaic world than those mountaineers and their wives, who were clad in the skins of animals. More Jews got in at every station. It seemed as if the train had an attraction for them, as if it were a magnet which dragged them from those solitudes which were not made for them. It seemed strange, a few minutes later, to see them get out at poor little stations just like those where they had got in, as if it would have been natural for the engine to take them on and on towards quite new countries. It was an unforgettable scene, that sight of Israel floundering through the mud along the railway line, under a cloudy sky relieved by gleams of sunshine, like a picture from the Old Testament! All those rugged surroundings of mountains, forests, and rocks, that grand though rather monotonous scenery interested me now much less than that black crowd with its eyes of fire and its boots so full of holes that one could often see the big toes sticking out, and clad in those long greasy coats. The further I traveled the more my surprise grew, until it became quite oppressive. In little towns where I stopped for a while, I visited the streets, the insanitary dwellings, the synagogues where God was importuned with indecent fury; I caught glimpses of lives which I could never have believed existed. Evidently here was something unique in the world, a scene for which I was unprepared, a sort of medieval St. Vitus' dance. What am I saying? It was a fragment, an old remnant of civilization dating back to Antioch, Solomon, King David, Nineveh, Babylon, and lingering on here in misery! In short, I cannot express the extreme amazement into which I was thrown at the sight of this uncouth type of humanity, which I seemed to have discovered even as Bougainville discovered the Kanakas. I found myself confronted by a spectacle of prodigious interest, which at once attracted and repelled me; I had put my hand into a nest which was still warm, and which gave me at the same time a sense of pleasant heat and of disgust. This morning at the Budapest railway station, the people I had before me were exactly like those I had met long ago on the banks of the Waag torrent and on the Galician plain. What were they doing in that stationary train? What were they waiting for in that grass-grown siding? They were just continuing their ordinary history. They were a tribe of those Jews who had immigrated into Hungary during the war, and of whom the government were trying to rid themselves at any price by re-expediting them en masse to their country of origin. But everywhere on the Romanian, Austrian, and Czecho-Slovak frontiers the same order has been given. The stationmasters refuse to allow them to leave the train or to continue their journey. "We do not know you, or rather we know you too well," they say to these pilgrims. "Return whence you came!" And philosophically the ghetto on wheels returns to Budapest. Thus it is that for several months these Jewish flocks have traveled up and down the lines, a new and quite modern edition of the wandering Jew of old days, in which the railway train has taken the place of Ahasuerus' staff.

As I waited for my express train to carry me hundreds of miles away from that strange old story, I walked along by the side of the pitiable caravan in those wretched railway carriages, which reminded me grotesquely of the shelters improvised in the sands of Egypt or on the banks of the Euphrates. Certainly it was not a cheerful sight—that teeming mass, without a shelter or home, who would have died of hunger had it not been for the Jewish Alliance, which sent them a little money and food. Still, on that railway siding, as in the Galician mud, and doubtless also, I imagine, in the deserts of the Nile or under the willow trees of Babylon, the same incredible vitality, the same surprising energy, not untinged with gaiety, emanated from that sordid swarm. These people appeared to be quite at home in the midst of their misery; they moved about, washed, and cooked without being any more affected by it than the geese of Galician villages who splash through the muddy ponds without soiling their plumage. My curiosity amused and in no way offended them, and I even flatter myself that in the dullness of that siding my presence was an agreeable interlude. What can they be thinking of as they follow me with their quick eyes? Perhaps they are only appraising the value of my overcoat or the leather of my shoes. But that would be to interpret in too vulgar a fashion all that lies behind those faces, which are so alert with intelligence and cunning. Perhaps what they are saying to me is: "Well, yes, look at us. We are well worth it. So much confidence in the midst of disaster is not seen every day. Here today, gone tomorrow. It matters little. The only important thing is to live. Today is not very brilliant, tomorrow will perhaps be radiant. Where are you bound for? Paris? How do you know that when you reach it you will not find us there also? Fortune is so strange. These old railway carriages without wheels and this train without an engine may take us there before you."

Their eyes, full of malice, seem to say this to me. And near me, like an echo, I hear the Christian's voice, who murmurs in accents of despair: "Yes, yes, look at them. Here today—tomorrow elsewhere. At home everywhere and nowhere. Always full of hope! The Turk on the hill of Buda was not more dangerous than this disheveled Jew, sitting there on his traveling bag. In Asia's last assault, we have been the defeated!"

ANTELOPE HILL
PUBLISHING

ENJOYED THIS BOOK?

TO READ MORE, VISIT US AT

ANTELOPEHILLPUBLISHING.COM

Printed in the USA
CPSIA information can be obtained
at www.ICGtesting.com
CBHW020431100224
4170CB00001B/3

9 798892 520072